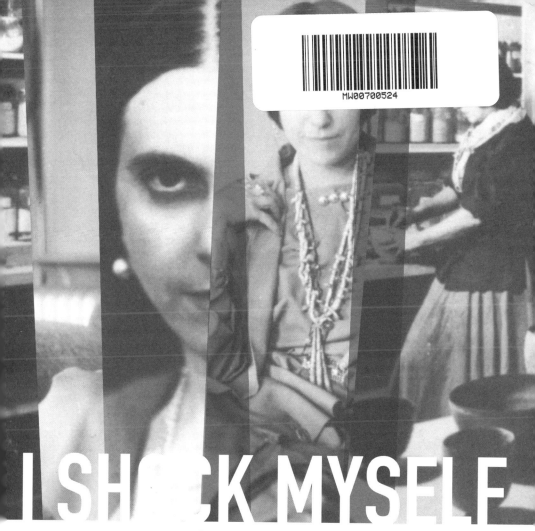

I SHOCK MYSELF

Beatrice Wood, Career Woman of Art

EDITED BY LINDSAY SMITH

4880 Lower Valley Road · Atglen, PA 19310

ISBN: 978-0-7643-5595-0
Printed in the United States of America

Library of Congress Control Number: 2018934599

Designed by Brenda McCallum
Cover design by Brenda McCallum

Cover photograph and p. 224 by Michael Chiabaudo

Published by Schiffer Publishing, Ltd.
4880 Lower Valley Road
Atglen, PA 19310
Phone: (610) 593-1777;
Fax: (610) 593-2002
E-mail: Info@schifferbooks.com
Web: www.schifferbooks.com

For our complete selection of fine books on this and related subjects, please visit our website at www.schifferbooks.com. You may also write for a free catalog.

Schiffer Publishing's titles are available at special discounts for bulk purchases for sales promotions or premiums. Special editions, including personalized covers, corporate imprints, and excerpts, can be created in large quantities for special needs. For more information, contact the publisher.

We are always looking for people to write books on new and related subjects. If you have an idea for a book, please contact us at proposals@schifferbooks.com.

Originally published: Ojai, CA: Dillingham Press. This new edition is reprinted from the Chronicle Books edition.

To D. Rajagopal, whose integrity and meticulous pursuit of perfection has helped me be aware of deviousness.

For a long time I hesitated writing about my life. For the mind is tricky, colors with infinite subtlety the ramifications of any act.

In the early part of my life, it is as if I made nothing but mistakes. I am convinced we would not be on earth, if we did not make mistakes; only through them do we learn. But through the bad I was always battling for the light.

"No" may be the most important word in the English language. Now near the end of my days, it falls glibly from my tongue.

Much protected in childhood, I wanted to know what the world was like, willing to pay any price to understand humanity.

I paid the price.

ACKNOWLEDGMENTS

While the substance of ceramics is clay and chemicals, the stuff of life is most certainly people. An autobiography, therefore, is essentially a big pot, shaped, designed, and filled by the people one has known and loved. Here is where the art of autobiography is as imperfect as that of ceramics, for how can I include all those who have added pleasure and sustenance to my life without creating a book the length of *War and Peace*?

In the last years, friends have been weaving in and out of my busy days, bringing encouragement, companionship, and delight. I am happy to mention a few of them here. Aina Taylor, with her morning phone calls, releases me from my self-imposed discipline of work, laughing with me over the fanaticism of religious-minded people who speak of higher life, yet hold no compassion or humor. A gifted artist, she has chosen instead to devote her energy to easing the woes of aging people.

I have been friends with Helen Merriam since I first moved to Ojai, California. She has practicality and a generous point of view which I very much admire. Connie Wash, an exquisite woman of elegance and charm, loves Ojai the way I do, and has the courage to speak up for the preservation of this beautiful valley. Dr. Joan Halifax, the extraordinary director of the Ojai Foundation, has inspired me with her energy and administrative ability. A medical anthropologist, she is one of the most intellectual women I know. Made of steel, she travels all over the world teaching and lecturing, and has so much energy, she runs up mountains others labor to climb. I could not have continued my workshop without the help of Lola Rae, a potter with more mechanical sense than myself, who spends hours taking care of the "donkey work" of my clay activity. A woman of strength, she is able to make and keep to swift decisions, never losing any of her femininity.

For years, my account books have been kept by Jay Reisinger, who in a protective manner continually reminds me that I have no money to spend on whims. We exchange insulting little notes full of double meaning and affection. Lyn Hebenstreit, a hardworking and attractive young man, and his wife, Suza, came into my life the same time Jay did. They were living in a trailer when it came time for Suza to deliver their first child, so they had their baby by natural childbirth in my home. A feud continues with my gardener, Alisdair Coyne, about how much water the cactus needs. I water them lavishly, while he protests this drowns the roots. Since they are blooming, I insist that I am right!

Twenty years ago Ram Pravesh Singh of India came into my life, and later came to Ojai to help me with my work. His son, Lallan, who lives in Utah, is married to an angelic woman, and they have three cherubic children. Lallan is close to my heart because of his wonderful sense of humor. I can always cry on his shoulder when his father, with his Oriental traditions, refuses to agree with my point of view.

Weekends have been enriched by visits from the beautiful and talented Helen Hooper McCloskey, who is married to Pete McCloskey, ex-congressman and a brilliant lawyer. Helen and I spend hours sharing politics and nonsense, trying to save the world. When she came across my manuscript about a trip I took to Holland in 1930, *The Angel Who Wore Black Tights*, with typical efficiency she sat down and had it published.

One of my dearest friends is Dorothy Stahl, whom I have known for fifty years. Though she lives far away and we meet rarely, a closeness prevails that endears her to me. Years ago she told me that she never told a lie; it made life simpler, for she never had to remember. This remark impressed me and I have tried to follow her example. Another friend, Rhea Case, also lives far away, but I can never forget the years she helped me through arduous times, showing herself to be a giving and intuitive person.

I have managed delightful friendships with two charming men: Bob Skiles and Brig. Gen. Henry Huglin. Bob lives in Big Sur, loves Japan, and is writing a book about its hidden temples. When I visit his home, he complains I wear him out by forcing him to dance the tango with me. Henry Huglin, a courageous pilot in World War II, says he is going to marry me in the next life. Here his courage fails him. What woman wants romance in the future?

I am indebted to Sarala Sharma, director of Indian crafts for the World Fair in Montreal, for teaching me an understanding of Indian folk art and its value. I am equally indebted to Arturo Schwarz—the noted Italian authority on Dada— for including several of my drawings in his beautiful and scholarly works on Marcel Duchamp and modern art. Paul Karlstrom, through his charm, inveigled me to give all my papers to the Smithsonian Institute, so now, while I am living, he knows all my sins and secrets and does not have to wait until I die. Lee Waisler—a fine artist—often has appeared to lift my spirits on dark days when the kiln comes out badly. He has encouraged me in drawing, and I am indebted to him for bringing out a collection of my etchings. Much of his time is spent working for world peace, protesting nuclear buildup, and using his art to express this concern.

Known for her superbly arranged exhibitions, it was my good fortune that Dextra Frankel not only arranged a retrospective for me, but also brought out a catalog that is a craftsman's dream. She found photographs of friends and my early work that I did not know existed. Dextra has become a legend for just this kind of quality in her work. Marlene Wallace, a noted photographer, lent photographs to the exhibition and has been consistently generous. She frequently prepares slides or prints for museum and gallery shows, often meeting overnight deadlines.

Mark Del Vecchio of Garth Clark Gallery, New York, visits Ojai, and flatters me that I am one of the few potters who can be depended upon to deliver work on time. He cleverly maneuvers me into making cups and saucers for the gallery, in addition to luster bowls and the figurative sculpture which I prefer making. Wayne Kuwada of Garth Clark Gallery, Los Angeles, also flatters, so I stay up nights getting ready for his arrival. He enjoys my naughty figures and always brings a chocolate cake when he visits, so I have promised to run off to Paris with him in the near future.

For a long time Francis Naumann, a friend and art historian, was interested in getting this book published. Through a circuitous series of events, it has finally come about. Bob Zaugh of Peace Press, whom I met when he arranged a series of interviews for me, also showed sympathy for getting the ball rolling. Bob, with his devious innocence and perceptive mentality, brought the project to life. Through him I met Lindsay Smith, my editor. Until I wrote a book, I did not understand why writers were always referring with appreciation to their editors. A writer needs an editor the way an actor needs a director. So it is with much admiration that I mention Lindsay, who brought wise suggestions, clarified obscure situations, and at all times, understood my way of thinking. She fills me with astonishment at what the American woman can do. With appreciation, I also mention Roger Conover of M.I.T. Press who, with his scientific mind, brought economy to the text and helped the story begin its journey. Also through Bob Zaugh I met Susan Grode, my legal advisor for the book. Susan is a highly successful lawyer with a background in art, who arduously protects her clients with a combination of astute legal sense and sympathetic understanding of the "artistic temperament." Bonnie Mettler of Peace Press brought her talent as art director to the fore, arranging photographs and drawings with consummate skill, and designing the overall layout of the book. I thank Chuck Ross for his fine insights and cooperation in proofreading the galleys, and also Susan Clark and Helen Friend, who in the early stages of writing this autobiography spent hours typing and editing, and encouraging me to continue.

One of the wonderful things in life is that new friends become old friends. Thus, in addition to the others, I mention Rick Dillingham. A talented and original potter, Rick took on the responsibility of publishing this, my story. Nothing could be more meaningful to me than having a colleague so supportive.

CONTENTS

Beatrice Wood, Untitled, 1989.
Pencil, pastel, and watercolor, 17" h x 11" w

FOREWORD

It was more than fifteen years ago when I first came across the name Beatrice Wood. She was the person identified in the company of Marcel Duchamp and Francis Picabia, in a frequently reproduced photograph of the three taken in Coney Island in 1917. Who was this wide-eyed, mysterious woman, I can recall wondering, who posed for this photograph, clutching onto the rim of an oversized hat while seated sidesaddle on the back of an artificial bull?

Her name was drawn to my attention again during the opening of the Duchamp retrospective at the Museum of Modern Art in 1973. I noticed that she was credited as the lender of an important early drawing entitled *Aeroplane*; the accompanying label read: "Collection Beatrice Wood, Ojai, California." Now my curiosity was piqued. Apparently this woman, who appeared in a photograph taken some fifty-five years earlier, was still living. How did she come to possess this drawing? Did Duchamp give it to her? Could she have been one of his lovers? Where was Ojai?

All of these questions would be answered during summer 1976, when I began assembling information for a book on the subject of New York Dada. Aided by one of the most reliable, yet often overlooked sources of scholarly information—the telephone directory—I discovered a listing for Beatrice Wood in California.

When I called, I was surprised and delighted to hear the voice of an alert, responsive, and quick-witted woman who, I guessed, had to be well into her eighth or ninth decade of life. She suggested I visit her on my next trip to the west coast.

Three weeks later, I was behind the wheel of a rented car, slowly climbing the one-mile vertical ascent of Highway 150, which overlooks the majestic Ojai Valley. Upon approaching her low-lying ranch style home and studio, perched atop a hill in the midst of a truly majestic landscape, I noticed an array of ceramic figurines poking their heads out from behind a well-kept terrain of cacti, rose bushes, and tropical plants. "This woman has got to be strange," I can recall mumbling to myself. With some trepidation I knocked on the door of her exhibition room, which, like the mailbox down the drive, was painted shocking pink. The woman who answered was dressed in an Indian sari and bedecked with an assortment of silver bracelets, rings, and other pieces of heavy, decorative jewelry. For a moment I thought that I might have wandered into the wrong place, but Beatrice quickly identified herself and within minutes, her charm and the ease of conversation proved immediate comfort, and made me feel as though I was visiting an old friend who I had not seen in years.

Initially, I was interested in knowing more about her relationship with Duchamp and the Arensbergs, the collectors of modern art she met in 1916, and with whom she had remained friends until their deaths in the early 1950s. But as our conversation progressed, I found myself wanting to know more about this enchanting woman and her own artistic production.

Her very career as an artist began as an act of defiance; while still in her teens she became so frustrated by the suffocating lifestyle of her wealthy family that she announced to her mother that she wanted to experience Bohemian life and paint in a garret. After several dreadful arguments, her mother finally relented and sent her young daughter off to Paris, where she attended drawing lessons at the famed Julien Academy. Her rebellious spirit would be further fueled a few years later in New York, where her encounter with two Frenchmen—Marcel Duchamp and Henri-Pierre Roché—changed the course of her life. Beatrice met Duchamp while visiting French composer Edgard Varese, who was hospitalized with a broken leg. At that time Duchamp was famous in this country as the painter of the *Nude Descending a Staircase*, the scandalous success of the 1913 Armory Show. Soon after their meeting, Duchamp introduced Beatrice to his good friend and compatriot Roché, a collector and diplomat, who was later in life to become a novelist. Together these two men not only shared a close and intimate relationship with Beatrice, but they also provided the encouragement and guidance that was crucial to her development as an artist.

Contradiction—if the word can be thought of in a positive sense—is the single most consistent unifying feature in Beatrice's artistic production. Whether she is sketching a figure, throwing a pot, or writing a story, she invariably forces a combination of extremely diverse visual elements into a single artifact, elements which in strictly formal terms are considered opposite, or mutually exclusive. For example, in her sketches, this unconscious impulse can take an elegantly rendered and highly controlled line and cause it to look like a child's scrawl on its other end, yet the resultant drawing ingeniously fuses these opposing techniques into a compatible reading of the whole. Critics have recognized this same quality in her ceramic works, which often combine elements borrowed from primitive or naïve sources with an elegant and highly sophisticated glaze that is many a potter's envy.

Just exactly how Beatrice accomplishes this remarkable fusion remains a mystery, but its source can be traced to her early friendship with Duchamp, and thus, though indirectly, to the nihilism of Dada, where contradiction often served as the very subject of inspiration. Whereas the Dadaists presented these elements without excuse, Beatrice consistently masks her creative message in an aesthetically charming package. The contrivance that could readily be associated with this procedure is entirely absent in her artistic production, and for that matter in her personality as well. Just ten minutes of conversation with this remarkable woman reveals a penetrating intelligence presented in the guise of whimsy and innocence.

Despite the romantic inclinations she delights in exhibiting, she possesses an innate pragmatism which has probably been the single most effective factor in determining her course of action throughout life. It was during a late-night walk together beneath the clear Ojai sky that Beatrice revealed to me the depth of her practicality—as well as her wit. Looking up at the blanket of stars covering us, I contemplated the futility of man's attempt to understand the sheer enormity of the universe. I confided to Beatrice my frustration in attempting to grasp the inconceivable notions of infinite space and eternity that have perplexed me since childhood. Finally, I concluded: "Maybe after we die we get to know the answers to these questions . . . maybe that's what heaven is." Beatrice looked at me thoughtfully, then smiled. "No, no, no," she chuckled. "If heaven is anything, it must be the great relief one experiences in no longer wanting to know the answers to such questions!"

Over the course of the last nine years our friendship has continued without interruption. Despite the three thousand miles that separate us we communicate continually, either over the phone or by mail. Anyone who has corresponded with Beatrice knows that she answers most of her letters by return mail, often embellishing her responses with delightful little illustrations.

As I once wrote Beatrice, one of the greatest revelations of our friendship was the discovery that I could share an important emotional, intellectual, and even spiritual rapport with someone whose age superceded mine by more than half a century!

She responded immediately, and her answer made it clear why I was unconscious of the years separating us:

Old people used to tire me with the terrible remark that they didn't feel old, and now I am going to tumble into the same remark and say, regardless of time, one does not feel old. The only mentor to bring one up to heel is the mirror. I wrestle with it every morning, and say to it, "No. No." Then I walk away from it and dance on the hilltops. If one can function, old age is a wonderful time of life. One sees patterns of one's conduct, the foolish bypasses into stupid behavior . . . Now I can lust after handsome young men, thinking it would be fun to go to Singapore with them, and since they have no idea what goes on in my mind, no mischief follows, no heartaches consume one, and one skips on to the next fine fellow who passes through the door. In spite of age, one can still escape into the romantic.

The concepts of infinity still confound me, but it is evident that Beatrice Wood embodies the quality of timelessness—right here on earth.

Francis Naumann
New York 1985

Marie T. Keller, "Francis and Beatrice", 1993

PART ONE

Beatrice Wood, *The Man Who Didn't Understand Women.*
Pencil, pastel, and watercolor, 1989, 17" h x 11" w

KISSED

The train whistled. While people crowded around one another sobbing goodbye, I wept for Maurice, beautiful beyond description in his uniform. He came close, took me in his arms, and put his lips on mine. Volts of electricity ran through me as I melted in his embrace. I was stunned at the ravishing pleasure it gave. Because it was a sensation I had never imagined, I was afraid I would now have a baby.

I watched the train disappear and heard the whistle grow fainter and fainter. There I stood, a forlorn figure, wondering how I was going to bring up the child. It was the eve of World War I, in Etretat, near Le Havre, France. I was in my teens, and the world glowed in a dream of romance. But the dream had nothing to do with reality. Reality was my rebellion against my mother, a dominating, aristocratic woman who devoted herself to protecting me from life—both its miseries and ecstasies. Determined I should remain a virgin—perhaps forever— she dressed me in lace, taught me to curtsy, and to remain silent unless spoken to. As my dear but rather passive father stood by, my mother and her two sisters, my aunts, attempted to turn me into a porcelain doll. But I was no doll beneath my childhood lace. At fourteen, my secret accomplices had been Dostoevsky, Tolstoy, de Maupassant, Colette, Shakespeare, Freud, and Oscar Wilde. I have no idea how I found out books by such writers existed, but I lost my virtue reading *Madame Bovary* by a spirit lamp.

I was full of curiosity about the world beyond. I would look at the stars and wonder why they did not fall down; I would watch myself falling asleep, trying to catch the moment that I left wakefulness for a dream state. Deep down I longed for the carefree life of an artist, and imagined living in a simple garret, free of pompous antique furniture. Artists were not interested in material things, as my mother's friends were. In the dark, secret dreams of my youth, I envisioned resting my head on a man's shoulder and leading an immoral existence, whatever that might be.

Every time I mentioned painting and living in a garret, my mother threatened suicide. I knew that I would have to run away from home. Finally, to appease me, I was sent to a small village in France, chaperoned by Miss Osborne, an elderly spinster of thirty whom I detested. Artists and peasants lived in the village of Giverny, with one tired horse and buggy as the town's only means of transportation. The great painter Monet, by then an old man, had his home and enchanting garden there. Once I peeked through the leaves and saw his glorious head with its white hair as he painted in his flower beds. His canvases looked exactly like the oils I had studied in the museums. I trembled as I spied on this master.

above: My mother and I, Paris 1903

left: Father

right: I was born radical. Even when I was a little girl, I had a feeling of antagonism toward my mother. My family used to look at me and say, "She doesn't belong to us. She's entirely different." | Fifteen years old, New York 1909

Miss Osborne agreed to start painting with me each morning at nine. She was not, however, able to organize herself. After three days of waiting, I set out for the fields alone. A few days later we quarrelled over a spider, so I picked up my gear and moved out to the inn where a few students and models lived. The owner did not want to accept me as a tenant, but my eager face, diminutive figure, and heavy paint box won him over. He confessed there was an attic left, reachable only by a ladder. It was a large space with a ceiling at uneven angles and small windows that allowed just enough light to create shadows, like in a Rembrandt painting. It was "full of promise."

At last! Alone with art, living in a garret like a real artist. This was paradise. I lifted my arms to the sky, picked up a paintbrush, and attacked the canvas. An outdoor scene in the morning, a still life in the afternoon, a fantasy at night. The walls quickly became lined with paintings, and more were stacked on the floor. All disasters. But it did not matter. I lived in an attic and was blissfully happy.

Everything would have been wonderful, except that Miss Osborne wrote my mother and soon, without notice, she arrived. A beautiful woman with great style, she came from a world of servants and Pierce Arrow cars; she did not approve of smocks and turpentine. Slowly she climbed up the ladder, her high heels clicking as she ascended, her black dress with tulle at the throat rustling, and the ostrich plumes on her French hat bobbing up and down. She had never been in an attic before.

Slowly she climbed up the ladder, her high heels clicking as she ascended.

As she surveyed the room full of the ghosts of Botticelli, Whistler, and Sargent, and dreams of gold medals from the Academy, I awaited her exclamation of approval at the evidence of my talent.

"How can you live in such filth?" she exclaimed, "Look at those cobwebs!"

Mother took me back to Paris. Two years later I tried to run away again. This time my mother consented to let me study with Gordon Craig in Italy. I was eighteen and mad to be an actress.

Gordon Craig was one of the great figures in theatre, the first to abolish stiff canvas scenery and replace it with curtains and footlights. I had read about him and knew my talent would blossom in the presence of such a great man. I went so far as to tell my mother that Gordon Craig was the son of Ellen Terry, one of the esteemed actresses of the nineteenth century— although I did not tell her that he was illegitimate, nor that he had fathered one of Isadora Duncan's children.

Mother exchanged proper correspondence with Mrs. Craig, the tuition fee was paid, and my railroad ticket was in my hands. Two days before my planned departure, some woman at the American Club in Paris filled my mother's ears with gossip.

Mother strode ominously into my room. "Did you know that Gordon Craig was an immoral man? You are not going. I have cancelled your reservation."

"But he has a wife there!" I meekly protested.

"I never heard of such a thing," and with a glance of fury she walked out of the room, shuddering as if I were a lunatic.

Throwing myself on the bed, I wept for twenty-four hours. Gone were my hopes for a creative and worldly mentor. So what if Craig was immoral? I had read that most men were immoral. Besides, since everyone had to be seduced once, I would rather be seduced by a wit than a dullard.

Once again I threatened to run away. Mother spoke of suicide. Finally she agreed that I could remain another year in Paris. Instead of the finishing school where she had put me the previous year, she arranged for me to live with an aristocratic family who had recently lost both sons in aviation accidents. They wanted a young person around to help fill their emptiness.

The moment I met Madame de Nieuport, I loved her. She was round like a chocolate drop, her white hair meticulously marcelled, and her handsome features made up to perfection. She was a Viscountess married to a colonel twenty years her senior. He had been head of St. Cyr—the French West Point—but now spent his days buried in the classics that lined his study. In his wrinkled sweater, his shrunken form stooped over a desk, he sat reading, trying to forget the tragedy of his two sons. Both had been famous aviators, inventors of the Nieuport airplane, and had been killed within a year of each other. I spent the following happy winter with the Nieuports, sleeping in a double bed with a canopy, gazing out the window at the Arc de Triomphe, and feeding the colonel's dog *pate de fois gras* when Madame's back was turned.

Anticipating my next rebellion, my mother arranged for me to study acting under Frances Duff, who had coached Mary Garden in her triumphant role in the opera *Louise*. Mary had worn a tight-fitting gown and moved with the grace of a leopard. Mother assured me that Miss Duff's liberal method of teaching—at the time she had no idea *how* liberal—would compensate for the loss of Gordon Craig.

I rode side saddle and he lifted me from my horse, holding me close to his heart.

She also found a diction teacher for me, and I labored hour after hour over every French consonant and vowel until I could speak French as well as a native. Mother even arranged for me to study privately with Mr. Leitner, a leading actor of the Comedie-Française, for she harbored the notion that my being an actress would not be so bad if I were acting in French. Monsieur Leitner was not very tall, except in his opinion of himself, and nothing could conceal his disgust at my heavy, high-laced gripper shoes and inhibited poses.

Frances Duff immediately took me under her wing. An elegant woman with lace at her wrists, she smelled deliciously of French scent and walked into a room with the grace of a swan on a lake. She taught that the diaphragm was the center of emotion and drilled me in breathing, walking, sitting down, falling down, getting up, and mastering broad, operatic gestures.

"You move like a stick, as if you had never been in love. How can you act, if you know nothing of men? You must dance, take up ballet, and learn the tango. It is important to know what it is like for a man to hold you close."

I was willing . . .

Together with Madame de Nieuport, Frances choreographed my days as if I were a courtesan. Both were loving tyrants. Madame—a coquette—dwelled in a world of high fashion and horse racing. She took me to dressmakers and would never let me out of the house without first checking to see if my hat was on at the right angle, my veil taut. I began resembling a professional—though I still did not understand exactly what the "profession" was. No wonder that when I took Frigette, the colonel's dog, for a walk in the Bois de Boulogne men tipped their hats and whistled. If my immaculate clothes did not give the impression of a courtesan, the dog did, for it was a hint of the metier.

I was taken to the threatre, the opera, and attended the first performance of Stravinsky's *Le Sacre du Printemps*. Scandalously innovative, half the audience booed the piece, while the other half cheered. I recall shouting, "Bravo!"

Madame de Nieuport and her daughter, the wife of Guimet, who founded the Oriental museum of that name, introduced me to the Faubourg St. Germain set, which few Americans ever entered. It was a rather elderly group, mostly titled, and I visited homes full of French furniture. A particularly gracious count who liked horseback riding often took me for canters in the Bois de Boulogne. I rode side saddle, and when we stopped at one of the restaurants for *un petit verre*, he lifted me from my horse, holding me close to his heart. With my adolescent romanticism I imagined he would defy his aristocratic family and the church to marry me. When spring came, Madame de Nieuport thought it would be nice for me to spend a month in Etretat, a seaside resort near Le Havre. There I met Fanny Fleurot, an American girl studying to be an actress who lived with her family in a villa by the sea.

She was tall, depressed in the wrong places, with faded hair and as much temperament as a wheat field on a hot day. Her parents lived in Paris, where they entertained diplomats from all over Europe. There were rumors that they were spies for America. But of far greater interest to me was the fact that Mrs. Fleurot wore a wig; it was rumored that she lost her hair in an unfortunate love affair that left her lover in a wheelchair. I did not understand why, but it was also whispered that a strange disease sometimes followed love. Fanny and I were left alone during the day to roam wherever we wished, to swim in the ocean, to eat enormous numbers of *petits gateaux*, to run up and down the boardwalk of the casino, and to join the company of a group of strolling actors who were soon to open in a play there.

That was how I met Maurice.

Maurice was a roving actor, currently attached to a blonde who played leading roles in this second-rate company. He had eyes like a dove and a full, lovely mouth. He suggested that I understudy the lead and be given a few lines to speak. I hinted that I had experience on the stage. In fact, I had been an extra for one performance in which Sarah Bernhardt played, and afterward met her in the dressing room. She had the bearing of a great stage actress, but with heavy mascara on her eyes was hardly alluring.

Maurice, sensing my inexperience, coached me. He helped me with lines and sometimes put his arm around me in the demonstrative manner of actors. This, of course, convinced me that he planned to dismiss his blonde, make me his leading lady, and develop my extraordinary talent.

Thus the days passed, full of gaiety and distraction. The play was to open in a few days, and at last I could proclaim myself a bona fide actress. The beaches and casino were crowded, the restaurants full, and the ocean continued its roar above the din of American tourists.

There was a bulletin board outside the casino that kept us informed about local activities. Three days before the opening of the play there was a notice that troops were mobilizing in central Europe. No one paid any attention to it.

Three days later, huge black letters jumped off the bulletin board announcing complete mobilization of all men.

War had been declared.

The town fell apart. American millionaires fled like rabbits, English tourists scurried off like chickens, and every Frenchman suddenly appeared in uniform. Shops closed, communications were cut off, and food became scarce.

The deserted casino was like a discarded picnic basket. Numb, I had no idea what to do. For the few of us remaining in town, food supplies were so short we subsisted on potatoes and fish. It was the end of July, and because my mother had been planning to come to France in early August, she did not send me my monthly allowance. I was stranded with seven dollars in my purse. Cable communications with America were severed; there was no way of knowing when they would be resumed.

My heart bled for France. I loved and felt closer to her than to America. In an effort to help lift her sorrow I joined the Red Cross and started making bandages. In the meantime, Madame de Nieuport wrote that I could stay in her apartment if I chose to return to Paris. The Fleurots insisted that it was out of the question for a young girl to travel on a train loaded with troops. Secretly I loved the idea.

"I cannot allow you to be near so many men," said Mrs. Fleurot emphatically. Mr. Fleurot, standing at the window, nodded in support of this statement.

"But I long to return to Paris. If she falls defeated to the Germans I will live there heroically, enduring defeat."

I heard Mr. Fleurot choke.

Not wishing to be a burden to the Fleurots, who had very little food, I insisted on moving to a small hotel nearby, where the sad-eyed innkeeper extended credit. Within three weeks communications were resumed with America and my parents sent several hundred dollars. I paid the hotel keeper and decided to return to Paris.

But the Fleurots had a more serious argument.

"Since you now have money, you must return to America as soon as possible."

"No."

They whispered, and reluctantly Mr. Fleurot took the initiative from his wife. "My dear child, you are a foreigner and too young to be here by yourself. We want you immediately to go to Le Havre and see when you can book passage back to America."

"I'll go if you wish. You know there isn't a chance of getting passage. Stranded Americans have swamped the steamship offices; millionaires are going steerage, sleeping on decks, and fighting with each other to do so."

Mrs. Fleurot broke in. "But you must show that at least you tried. We cannot be responsible for you." Whereupon Mr. Fleurot pounded his fists on the table: "I agree with every word my wife says."

The next morning, to placate them, I arose at six a.m. and took the stagecoach to Le Havre. It was exhilarating to mount the high steps of the fragile coach—the only means of communication at that time—and watch the two nervous horses waiting to start on the road. We had to pass through the lines, and anything could happen—even death, for with thousands dying, why should I be spared? Soldiers were everywhere, sentries stood along the road, and I could hear the sound of cannons in the distance. This was adventure. For two hours the coach rolled over the narrow road, skirting lovely hills and revealing glimpses of the ocean, as if the unspeakable horror was not taking place. Several times we were stopped by troops and, breathlessly, I gazed out of the window, hoping a soldier would grab me and try to get secrets from me, as if I were a spy. To my disappointment nothing happened.

We arrived at Le Havre, and I went directly to the shipping office. Furious that the Fleurots were forcing me to make this foolish effort, I walked in and asked the clerk for passage. A dilapidated middle-aged man wearily told me that there were no passages to be had at any price. I explained that I had money to pay, but he grumbled that diamonds could not buy passage.

Having done my duty, I skipped off to pay respects to the American consul. Then my obligations to the Fleurots would be completely fulfilled. The consul was a charming man, with twinkly blue eyes and a natty tweed suit. He motioned me to sit down, acting as if he had all the time in the world.

In one of my many fashionable French hats

"What can I do for you?"

"I am an American, but I speak perfect French and I have money, so I can take care of myself. I have tried to get passage back to America and there are no reservations." I smiled with delight and continued, "Now I put myself at your service. I love France and will do any kind of work. I will translate, make bandages, care for the wounded, go to the battlefield, anywhere you wish to send me." My notion of caring for the wounded was sitting near good-looking patients, dreamy-eyed, holding their hands.

His eyes blinked as he gently asked, "Don't you want to go home? I'm a grandfather. I'm sure your parents want you home."

"How my parents feel has nothing to do with this situation," I nervously protested. "France is in trouble. I am here to help her." Then folding my hands with finality, I announced, "Anyway, there are no passages to be bought at any price, so now I am free to go wherever I am needed." Heroically I tossed my head, knowing I was appointed to aid the cause of France.

The consul patted my hand soothingly, "My dear, you must, nevertheless, return. I will see that you get passage." He continued with amusement, "If there is one thing the American government does not want, it is a girl your age helping an army win a war."

A young attache took my arm, led me to a consulate carriage, and off we went to the steamship office, where I turned in my note from the consul. Upon reading it, a man opened a desk drawer, took out a clip, and put two papers together, stating flatly, "Here is a reservation for you. Today is Thursday, you sail Saturday. We have given you an outer state room on the upper deck."

My heart sank.

I, who wanted danger, adventure, and love.

Having nothing to do until the evening when my coach returned to Etretat, I sauntered along the beach. It was crowded with soldiers on leave, each with a girl, many embracing. I sat alone on the vast sands, my golden hair waving in the breeze, and contemplated my unhappiness.

The Fleurots were finishing dinner when I arrived home that night. Mrs. Fleurot was pouring coffee and, in spite of my despair, I noticed her wig was on crooked.

"I have passage," I announced morosely. "The consul arranged it."

"Really?" Neither paid any attention to my significant words.

"Yes. I leave Saturday."

"Come on, stop joking, tell us what happened. Did you have any luck at all?" Mr. Fleurot asked heartily.

"Yes, I tell you, I have passage." I hated his guts. "The consul arranged the ticket. I leave the day after tomorrow."

I burst into tears, blew my nose, opened my purse, and showed them the ticket. They were as impressed as I was disappointed.

Saturday morning I boarded the boat. Other Americans crowded the docks, screaming with joy that they were going home. I stood at the railing, hanging on to a last glimpse of France. None of my compatriots cared what happened to her. France was bleeding and they played the banjo.

The ship began to move away from the pier; slowly fog came down like a grey curtain, shutting out my beloved land. I wanted to stop the boat and get off.

I heard someone whisper, "We won't be out of danger until tomorrow. The waters are full of mines."

I hoped we would strike one.

I Become an Actress

It took a year to get used to New York. I resented America's indifference to the war in Europe, its carefree ways, and frivolous parties. My mother hoped I would give up the idea of acting, but after my two years of study abroad, I was determined to prove myself on stage. My ambition had shifted from being the great woman painter of the age to becoming the great actress of the day.

Having studied in Europe with teachers from the Comédie-Française, and still wearing my beautiful clothes, I had no trouble getting into the French Repertory Company, which was then being organized in New York. It appeased my mother to have me act in French. I was told, however, that a lady's maid must accompany me to rehearsals and wait in my dressing room while I was on stage. Oh, God! I was underage.

The actors hated me, and I did not blame them. It was rumored that my father was a millionaire and had bought my way in, that I was the sweetheart of a politician, the favorite of the manager . . . none of this was true. My father was in real estate and we were comfortably well-off, but not rich, and I was still as pure as Ivory soap. I hated the lady's maid as much as my fellow actors did, but was too timid to say anything.

I loved the backstage atmosphere. The hours spent in dingy dressing rooms and the continuous morning and afternoon rehearsals never seemed arduous. I was proud that I had become a professional.

I wish I could say I was good, but except for my youth and beautiful clothes, I was ineffectual. From 1914 to 1916, I played more than sixty parts, but in only one of them did I move the audience. It was a love scene—of course—with the company's leading man, Reuben. He was the only actor who ever paid any attention to me, although he was the real-life lover of the leading lady. Each time we played our love scene the audience responded loudly to the passionate vibrations, while the leading lady stared with beady eyes from the wings.

One afternoon Reuben invited me to his apartment in the heart of the theatre district. I arrived drenched in perfume, wearing a soft blue suit and a white velvet hat trimmed with ermine tails. I had longed for this encounter, but suddenly I was embarrassed to be alone with him. His badly furnished room faced a dreary court and seemed sordid to me.

Sitting astride a chair, Reuben lit a cigarette, slowly eyed me from top to bottom, and smiled at my discomfort. It did not take him long to put his arms around my waist and murmur seductively in French: "*Je veux entre dans toi.*" I was sure he was saying something he should not, but not sure what. I stared at him indulgently, my eyes pools of innocence, and wondered what to do next.

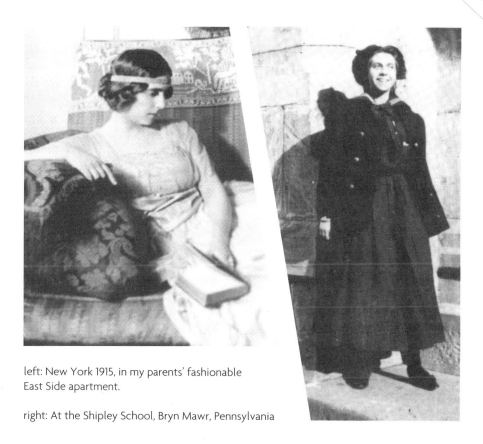

left: New York 1915, in my parents' fashionable East Side apartment.

right: At the Shipley School, Bryn Mawr, Pennsylvania

My virtue was saved by the telephone, which he picked up with a scowl. I could hear the shrill voice of his suspicious mistress, and when he hung up he had the air of a little boy caught in mischief. I quickly exited, sparing us both a poorly acted love scene.

However, our onstage embrace inspired someone to write my mother—anonymously—that I was having an affair. "In public life we cannot avoid gossip," I told her with regal dignity. Nevertheless, when the repertory season was over, she insisted that I make a social debut and begin my life in earnest.

Finally, the horrid day could no longer be put off. I wore a pale blue taffeta dress and a Juliet cap with pearls in my hair. Four of my schoolmates, Marion Cleveland, daughter of President Cleveland, Beatrix and Constance Buel, and my best friend, Elizabeth Reynolds, stood in line with me while a small orchestra played. The conversation was a sugar bowl of triviality. I was impatient if one could not discuss world starvation in the first sentence. Annoyed and arrogant, I fled to my room, locked the door, and wept. Mother missed me and commanded my return to the receiving line, where I wore a frozen smile through the rest of the evening.

Mother simply could not make me the popular debutante she wanted. I was the flop of the season. People invited me to parties and I would not talk. I was too timid for small talk, and the only subjects that interested me were art and literature. All businessmen were pitiful sloths sunk in materialism, and I refused to hold conversations with them. I was so naïve about social customs that when a Wall Street tycoon, whom my mother hoped I would marry, took me to the Plaza Hotel for dinner, I volunteered to pay part of the check. I was accustomed to artists who had no money.

Part of my social awkwardness was my mother's own fault, for she had never allowed me to play with other children. Summer vacations were spent in Europe, where I was dragged by a governess through museums; winters were spent at private girls' schools—Shipley and Finch—where the absence of boys was a fact of life. I was so painfully shy that when confronted by any young man I would withdraw into myself like a hedgehog and answer only "yes" or "no" to perfectly innocent and friendly questions—whereupon the gentleman would promptly walk away.

After one such encounter I rushed sobbing in humiliation to my dear friend, Elizabeth Reynolds, who had roomed with me at Ely Court. "I am a social monstrosity! I haven't the least idea what to say to a man!"

Elizabeth was working at petit point. Her hair, long and naturally wavy, shone as the sun struck it. She looked up and laughed.

"It's easy! Make a list of eight subjects, anything you like—trains, boats, dresses, dogs, cats—and start a conversation around any one. Before you know it, the ball will be rolling."

The next time a man took me to dinner, I considered a dozen subjects, unsure which one to choose until I noticed the wristwatch he was wearing.

I ventured timidly, "Is that a Swiss watch you are wearing?"

"No, but my uncle has one, a beauty from Geneva."

"Do Swiss watches have more jewels than American ones?"

I could hardly believe how well the system worked, for my escort began pouring out stories about his family and their clocks and pewter.

From that moment on I realized that any subject was as good a starter as any other. One could tie the world together if only one asked about the jewels in a watch!

It was not the first time that I sought and received excellent council from Elizabeth Reynolds. She was a great influence in my life and remained so until she died, many years later, when we were both old ladies. We met when I was twelve, she eleven, as students at Ely Court, the most fashionable finishing school of the day. In spite of the fact that the school was in Manhattan where my family lived, my parents had enrolled me as a boarder because they fought terribly and did not want me to witness their battles. To my mother's horror, I gained a reputation for being a bad influence on my schoolmates, though I never broke a single rule. I refused to study subjects I did not like—algebra, geometry, German grammar, and Latin— and proudly sat through those courses doing nothing, a smile on my face. Fortunately, I excelled at the subjects I did like, primarily literature and history, and at fourteen began reading extensively and collecting fine books. James McNeil Whistler's *Gentle Art of Making Enemies* was my bible.

Elizabeth Reynolds in costume, ca. 1916

Elizabeth's mother, an aristocratic woman of great warmth but modest income, had become house mother at the school. Because I was impressed with Elizabeth's poise and the sight of her lovely hair tossing in the wind as we played, I consented to be her roommate. We quickly became devoted friends. Though we were separated for years afterward, a week never went by that she did not write, and her friendship stood by me during my bleakest moments.

At twenty, she was teaching Russian at Columbia University, the first person in America to teach the language. She saw the Russian ambassador continually and translated numerous diplomatic documents. Throughout our school years together Elizabeth saw to it that I met interesting people. She introduced me to Isadora Duncan, who shocked a generation by appearing barelegged in Grecian gowns at a time when respectable ladies pretended to swoon at the glimpse of a thigh. When I met her she was rather flabby, not the spellbinder of the stage. She asked me to do tie-dying for her, and was pleased with the colors I used. She also invited me to a large party, where she appeared in a green ball gown, sadly drunk. Friends were sympathetic, understanding her grief over the loss of her two beautiful children who drowned when the car in which they were sitting slid into the water. Isadora never recovered.

Elizabeth also introduced me to the incomparable Anna Pavlova. As I watched her rehearse I was amazed at the fire and energy she brought to her work. She was wearing the scantiest chiffon costume, and the tiny muscles in her body looked like steel, as they shone under the sweat that poured off from her effort.

left: Mother relented and let me join Charles Coburn's play, *The Yellow Jacket*. New York, 1916.

right: Clustine, Pavlova's choreographer, taught me Russian folk dances.

She was truly magnificent, with a movement of the head and shoulders that no other dancer could touch. I also met Nijinsky, who had the genius of standing perpendicular, in elevation, and touching stillness. No other dancers have reached the heights of these two; they were dancers from another world.

Elizabeth even arranged for Pavlova's choreographer, Ivan Clustine, to teach me two Russian folk dances. It was quite an honor, as I was the only person outside Pavlova's company he was willing to coach. He supervised the making of two elaborate costumes I wore and arranged for me to dance for Nijinsky himself—who politely sat through my performance.

I danced for charity affairs and ambassadors, and then was asked to dance professionally for the Barrerre Little Quartette, a well-respected musical ensemble. I was to be paid $125 a night for two dances—a good sum in those days.

Upon hearing of this, my mother reacted in her characteristic manner. "No daughter of mine will be a professional dancer!"

Socially, in her mind, dancers were even lower than actors.

At this time I was also taking acting lessons with Yvette Guilbert, who had been the toast of France at the turn of the century. Famous for her costume—a tight black dress and long gloves—I was disappointed when she came into the room to greet me wearing a plain dark dress and no makeup. Furthermore, her bearing was as stilted and authoritative as that of the actors from the Comedie Française. Guilbert was an extraordinary chanteuse and best known for her naughty songs. These were what I wanted her to teach me! Instead she kept me studying classical roles. "Listen, my little one," she explained. "If you can master Racine, which is like moving big rocks, you will find everything that comes after much easier."

above: Norman Hapgood, editor of *Collier's*

below: Elizabeth Reynolds Hapgood

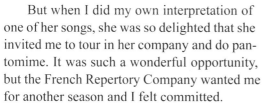

But when I did my own interpretation of one of her songs, she was so delighted that she invited me to tour in her company and do pantomime. It was such a wonderful opportunity, but the French Repertory Company wanted me for another season and I felt committed.

Another well-known figure I met through Elizabeth was Norman Hapgood, editor of *Collier's* magazine and a close friend of President Woodrow Wilson. He was a liberal thinker and a renowned drama critic. When he was not smiling his features resembled a hillside that had been neglected, but he had one of those appealing, homely faces that held charm and beauty in its bony structure.

Elizabeth, Norman, and I often dined together. Norman took us to meet William McAdoo, a son-in-law of President Wilson, and I sat tongue-tied in the presence of such a famous person. We also had tea with Charles Crane, a multi-millionaire, and a great figure during World War I; he was responsible for saving the people of Serbia from starvation by sending boatloads of food into their country.

Charles Crane invited Elizabeth and I to visit his estate in Woodstock, New York. Crane had the affable assurance of an elderly rich man, while his pleasant wife seemed to fade into the Louis XV furniture that filled their home. The house itself was designed by Frank Lloyd Wright and run by at least fifty servants.

Elizabeth told me he had other estates, equally well-staffed, with autos and chauffeurs on call in several cities. But Crane was no prisoner of wealth; he had a keen interest in European affairs and was drawn to Eastern philosophy, a subject which at the time held no attraction for me.

It was on the grounds of the Crane's luxurious home that Elizabeth asked me to take a walk with her. "I want to tell you something that I have not told a soul, not even my mother." She took my arm and we walked a few steps in silence. Then she said, "Norman and I are engaged." I knew they were seeing a great deal of each other, but it never occurred to me they were in love. Besides, he was twenty-seven years her senior.

Three months later they were married. I tore to their wedding from rehearsal, still in stage costume. As a bride Elizabeth took my breath away. She wore a Russian type headgear and looked like an angel. Theirs was a successful and happy marriage, lasting twenty years until his death.

Both Elizabeth and Norman were sympathetic to my desperate need to escape my mother's grasp and did everything possible to help. Norman gave me letters of introduction to present to the great actresses of the day—Minnie Maddem Fiske, Elsie Ferguson, and others. They offered me good parts, but mother would not let me accept anything except a starring role. She insisted I play the lead or nothing. I argued that I had no real experience, but she remained adamant: no daughter of hers would act unless her name were up in lights. Each time I would turn to Norman for consolation and he would give me more letters.

One day I received a letter from a Polish count who, using Norman's name, asked me to meet him at a well-known theatrical office. I rushed to see what he had to offer. Count Rodwan, the greatest and most scientific hypnotist in the world, sat me down in a comfortable chair and explained that he was hunting for a young and beautiful woman to hypnotize into being the finest actress of the day. This, I thought, was right up my alley. At last, I would be able to get away from home and be the greatest actress alive!

He tested my voice, marvelled at its tone, and admired my peerless grace. I was more and more impressed with him, as well as with myself. After I recited—in French—a fable of La Fontaine, he announced that at last his search was ended. I was his rapturous choice.

"We will begin rehearsals at once," the count declared. "How much money will you need to live on until the play is produced? I am prepared to pay you well." He approached, and his eyes held a strange gleam, as if he were going to hypnotize me on the spot.

"But I don't need money," I answered in a low voice, as if ashamed. I had been taught never to discuss money with people. "I have money; I live at home."

I never heard from the count again. Norman had no idea who this count was, nor how he had gotten either of our names. I have often thanked my guardian angels for protecting me from my own foolishness. I was willing to do anything

left: Helen Freeman, who was to become a lifelong friend.

right: *Sunwise Turn*

that would release me from the iron hold of my mother, even if it meant giving myself up to the grasp of another!

Shortly after that experience I met Helen Freeman, who was to become another lifelong friend. She was an actress, and one of the most beautiful women in New York, with radiant blonde hair, alabaster skin, and a sinewy body that was the dream of any dressmaker. She made countless speeches to raise money for the Theatre Guild, which probably would never have opened without her support. At her urging, I joined this idealistic and cooperative venture. For its first production I played a small part with only two lines. After having played leading ingenues in the French theatre this was something of a come-down. However, during the run of the play I shared a dressing room with Edna St. Vincent Millay. She was tiny and elf-like, with bright, gleaming eyes and reddish hair, and there was an air of mischief about her. I heard she did not get along well with women, but I found her delightful. Sitting next to each other at our makeup tables, we chatted easily. We were each careful, however, to keep our men in our own makeup kits. You might say we were impersonal about our personal relationships. Her personality was like her poetry—full of smiles and lightness. There was a lyrical quality to her voice and her movements, though this did not project itself onto the stage. She was probably too intellectual to be a good actress. On stage it is the emotions that win, not the mind.

The guild was a good experience, but I resigned after the play closed. My ego could no longer bear being treated like an extra!

In this period I frequented an establishment called Sunwise Turn, one of the first small, intimate bookshops in New York. It was founded by Mary Mowbray-Clarke and Madge Jennison, who read every book they sold. They held poetry readings where writers could meet and read manuscripts. I recited Amy Lowell's "Patterns" one evening, enraptured by the music of my own voice. Applause was polite.

top: Mary Mowbray-Clarke
top right: Mowbray-Clarke
below: Ananda Coomaraswamy, ca. 1916
below right: Ranta Devi

Mary and her husband, sculptor Mowbray-Clarke, were the first to desert New York for Rockland County. Many literary people soon followed, including playwright Maxwell Anderson and Henry Poor, the distinguished potter. It was an inspiration to visit the "Brocken," as Mary and Mowbray-Clarke called their country place. I often journeyed there on weekends to enjoy the lively conversation amid rural surroundings. They opened a door to a new world for many. It was there that I met Ananda Coomeraswamy, the renowned Indian scholar, who came up to Rockland County for a performance of *MacBeth* that we put on in Mowbray's studio. At that time I had no interest in India—although later it was to mean so much to me—nor any appreciation

Henri-Pierre Roché

of Coomeraswamy as a scholar. He was a commanding figure, tall with black hair, pale face, prominent nose, and a deep voice that carried a caressing accent. He had recently been divorced from his first wife, Ranta Devi, an Englishwoman and accomplished singer. Behind closed doors more sympathy was expressed for her than him, for he was overt in his attention to the ladies. I do not remember if I flirted with him—I probably did. He gave me a deluxe copy of his *Dance of Shiva*, and I wrote an illustrated murder story for him. He later became the esteemed director of Eastern art at the Boston Museum of Fine Arts, but by that time I had lost track of him.

"For instance, I was a little frightened of you the night you dined at my parents' home . . . I had the misfortune to make a vulgar remark in front of my mother, who did not understand, and you turned white with horror." from *POUR TOI* (For Thee—Adventures of a Virgin) Illustrated letters to Henri-Pierre Roché, 1917

In the meantime, Mary, thinking her husband a genius, promoted him like a perfect artist's wife. Mowbray evidently tired of being promoted, for one day he ran off with a quiet girl who was not at all interested in furthering his career. Mary, in spite of her flaunted liberalism, would not yield to a divorce. Mowbray lived happily ever after with the young woman without clerical sanction, a whispered scandal in those days.

Another good friend was Alissa Frank, a journalist. Dumpy but jovial, very well-read and Bohemian, she lived in New York's Greenwich Village. I enjoyed my visits to her simple apartment, where we would sit in front of the fireplace and spend hours discussing books and world problems. She knew artists and writers, and I envied her independence and sophistication.

One day I invited her to dinner at my parents' house. They regularly held open house on Sundays. We rarely sat down to dinner without sixteen at the table, with bountiful amounts of turkey, candied sweet potatoes, and homemade ice cream. Alissa came in rather shabby tweeds and I saw my mother observing the way her hair was cut. I was proud to introduce her to my family, but after her second visit my mother stated, "She is common. You should not have friends like that."

Once again my mother displayed her usual lack of empathy for the people and things that mattered to me. Her critical, judgmental nature would continue to drive me away—and it finally did for good.

I met a Frenchman by the name of Henri-Pierre Roché. He was tall, with keen eyes and a large nose dominating his narrow face. He was cultivated, well-travelled, and worked in the French diplomatic service. He was a writer, as well as an art collector. One of the first to collect modern art, he bought the works of Pablo Picasso, George Braque, and Constantin Brancusi before anyone else did. Roché had also travelled extensively in India and been art advisor to a maharajah.

I invited Roché to Sunday dinner. He conversed easily with my mother and other guests, and fit in so well I actually relaxed and had a good time. Besides, he was much more interesting than the stockbroker my mother was conniving to have me marry.

After Roché's visit, Mother came into my room and said, "You are falling in love with that man!"

Too shy to dare acknowledge such a thought, I was shaken that a secret part of me should be so violently invaded by my accusing mother. The next time Roché phoned, asking to call, I casually replied, "This time I'll come see you."

Taken aback, he protested, "But I live in a very simple room."

"I don't mind."

He hesitated. Frenchmen respect *jeunes filles*. Besides, he had been entertained by my family and was too much of a gentleman to take advantage of the situation. Yet, in certain circles only "loose" women were on the stage. He must have been puzzled.

My mother's remark had made me wonder if I *was* in love with him. I did not know . . . I found him sympathetic, but only as a friend. At forty, he was far too old for me. However, I refused to let my mother interfere in my friendships. I quickly thought of an excuse to tell him. "I have some shopping to do near your place, so I will come by."

I took the subway and walked two blocks to his address. He had a large room in a basement that opened onto the street; it had its own separate entrance and was like a private apartment.

He let me in without a fuss and watched as I stood taking in the fine books on the table, the single rose on his bureau, and the meticulous order of the small objects about the room. The late afternoon sun came in through cheap window curtains and transformed them into gossamer webs. The room was luminous and calm—and so was I as Roché stood there, his gentle and compassionate eyes caressing my face.

I stood motionless for a time, not knowing what to do or say. He did not move either. Finally, I pointed to the wall and said, "That is a nice drawing," then giggled out of embarrassment.

"An early Marie Laurencin," he said, looking at me steadily. "Come, take off your hat."

"No . . . I think I will keep it on . . ." I replied, clinging to it as protection against myself.

He took a step closer. "Then I will take it off." I wanted the sensation of happiness that came over me to last forever. I lowered my eyes and smiled. The next move was up to him.

Without another word we were in each other's arms. I offered no resistance. He carried me to the bed. "But you are a virgin. I must not ruin your life. I love you. We will lie here and I will think what to do. I would marry you, but I cannot."

"I have never believed in marriage," I murmured.

"I would marry you all the same," he replied tenderly. "But before we go further, I must tell you something." He paused, and took his arm from around my waist. "You should know that for twenty years I had a mistress in Paris. The last five years we have not lived together; we are like brother and sister. I cannot marry her, because she comes from a lower class, but she is a sweet, good woman and I cherish her. She understands I must be free, but it would kill her if I married someone else."

Henri's loyalty to another woman three thousand miles away was not a problem for me. I felt an affection toward her and included her presence in our magical circle.

And magical it was. I was loved by a man of tenderness and passion, unequalled in understanding and consideration. Older than myself, at times he acted like a *vieux-papa*, talking to me for hours about art. Often we had dinner in his room. We made a wonderful vegetable soup together, served with dark peasant bread and cheese. From the beginning we behaved like an old married couple. Every remark was surrounded by the unspoken language of love. If he said, "The knife is there," it meant, "I adore having you near." If I answered, "Where is the butter," it meant, "I waited more than twenty years for this to happen and it is more wonderful than I dreamed." He took me everywhere with him. We had gay dinners at bistros or big hotels. We talked and talked—as if we could

never find time to tell each other all the things that mattered. He was excited by the quality of my mind. "When you are an old lady, you will talk just like you do now. You will never age, and I will never tire of listening to you. You have something untouchable. Events of all kinds will happen around you, but they will roll off like water on a duck's back."

Roché, like a *vieux-papa*

He insisted that I become an artist; it was he who encouraged Marie Laurencin, and he was sure I had a talent as great as hers. I did not care about being an artist; I was only interested in love. Roché had released me from prudish views about sex, and made it a loving and creative experience. He impressed upon me: "It is important for a woman to have a fine relationship with a man the first time, for it marks her for the rest of her life."

I have often thought back on that statement, and always with gratitude to him.

A Second Great Love Comes into My Life

One day I was having tea in Alissa's apartment. It was cold out, but the fire inside was cozy and warm. The tea, with its dash of rum, made for easy conversation.

"You know," Alissa began like a good mama, though she was only eight years my senior. "You and Roché are beautifully suited to each other. You belong together. You have bloomed and grown since you met him. He is a wonderful man. You are lucky he is so fond of you." As she nibbled on her piece of toast, I felt her studying me. I knew something devious was going on in her mind. I studied the tea leaves in my cup.

"But there is another Frenchman in town you ought to meet," she continued in her husky, cajoling voice. "He is twenty-six and a musician."

"Not interested."

"But he is lonely."

"I know nothing about music."

"He is in a hospital without friends. There is nobody to speak French with him. He had an accident and broke his leg. You must go see him." She was curiously insistent.

"What would I say to him?"

"Anything! That you are pretty, young, and speak French is enough."

That was how I met Edgard Varèse, the brilliant avant garde musician who had recently arrived in the United States. I found him in a bleak hospital room. The walls were high and grey, and the room so empty it was like a cell. I knocked timidly on the open door, hesitating to enter. Then I saw a young man with one leg in a cast; the other was sticking out from under his sheet, naked and hairy. I was embarrassed. His young face was surrounded by an unruly beard, but his dark eyes flashed with relief when he realized I spoke his language.

Varèse greeted me warmly, taking in my fashionable French suit as I entered and sat down. He was surprised to hear I was an actress; neither my voice nor my countenance belonged to an

Edgard Varèse

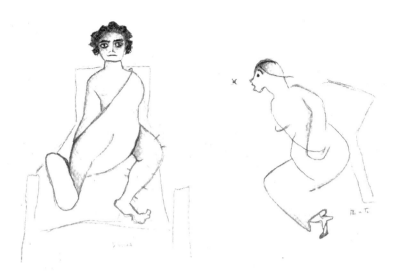

I had my mouth open, and a fly flew in.

actress. He wanted to know all about New York, especially about the city's musical life. He was discouraged that he had met so few people and they all had trouble understanding him!

I returned the next week for another visit. This time he told me about the difficulties he had trying to interest people in his revolutionary musical scores. He described the instruments he had invented and the tonalities he was trying to bring to his compositions. "I used streetcar gongs, pipes, bells, and things like that, for it is the music of the city, the soul of the city breaking into sound." He made quick, impatient gestures as he spoke.

"Can't you buy instruments to make the sounds that you want?" I asked, trying to be intelligent.

He scowled and threw his pillow on the floor. No one understood what he was doing, he roared. Americans were bourgeois!

"When you are out of the hospital, I will see that you meet certain people in the theatre," I said, trying to comfort him. "Alissa knows many interesting people and . . ."

Just then an embarrassing thing happened. Mid-sentence, a buzzing fly flew into my open mouth. I did not know what to do: spit it out, cry for help, or faint. No well-brought-up girl could spit in front of a man and I was too embarrassed to make my dilemma known. And so I swallowed the fly, alive and batting its wings. I have probably eaten stranger things since, but at the time I felt sure I was the only person in the world dutiful enough to swallow a live fly in the name of propriety.

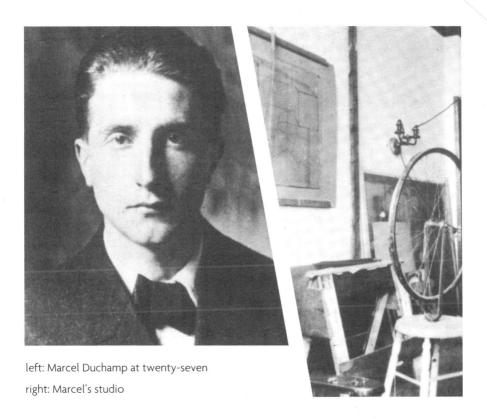

left: Marcel Duchamp at twenty-seven

right: Marcel's studio

On my third visit to see Varèse my life was to change, for Marcel Duchamp was there. The most celebrated painter of his day due to the sensational success of his *Nude Descending a Staircase*. Marcel at twenty-seven had the charm of an angel who spoke slang. He was frail, with a delicately chiseled face and penetrating blue eyes that saw all. When he smiled the heavens opened. But when his face was still it was as blank as a death mask. This curious emptiness puzzled many and gave the impression that he had been hurt in childhood.

Though I was delighted to know a man as masculine as Varèse, my attention changed the moment I met Marcel. Immediately he addressed me as *tu*, the French familiar of "you," used only with friends, family—or lovers!

When Marcel and Varèse launched into a discussion on modern art, I shrugged my shoulders and put in: "Anyone can do such scrawls."

Marcel replied wryly: "Try."

Back at home I sketched *Marriage of a Friend*, a tortured abstraction. Marcel liked it so much he published it in a small avante garde magazine, *Rogue*. Edited by his good friend, Alan Norton, *Rogue* was a revolutionary sheet in 1916. Gertrude Stein wrote a few lines for it.

"Why don't you paint?" Marcel asked me. "You can't always be so busy rehearsing?"

Marriage of a Friend

Varèse frowned, as he always did when the conversation drifted off the subject of music.

"No room at home."

"Then come to my studio. Often I am away. Come once, twice a week. Phone first, so I can tell you if it is all right. I'll be frank with you. There may be times when I don't want you to come."

From then on, whenever I had a free afternoon, I phoned and asked whether the studio was free. He would usually tell me to come over; if not, I assumed a lady was with him. Marcel did very well in that department, although friends laughingly told me that Marcel's lady friends were usually quite homely. Marcel later commented that unattractive women made love better than beautiful ones. Sex and love, he explained, were two very different things. I did not know what he was talking about.

Marcel's square room looked out onto a narrow court, facing the back of the apartment. A double bed, usually unmade, filled one alcove. There were two chairs, generally covered with clothes, and canvases in disorder everywhere. On the windowsill lay boxes of crackers and packages of Swiss chocolate, his regular diet. The room gave the impression of being in various stages of undress.

After the crowded luxury of my parents' home, I found this chaotic space an oasis of peace. Marcel knew I was in love with his good friend Roché and did not approach me amorously. Secretly I wished he would. My love for Roché could not keep me from being a little in love with Marcel, for he was a most charming man, with a devastating smile. I found myself dreaming about him all the time.

Marcel and his familiar pipe

If Marcel was out when I came, he would leave the key for me. If he was in his studio, he sat quietly in a chair with his legs crossed, smoking a pipe, and watched me passively as I worked. Then, at the end of the afternoon he quickly surveyed my sketches, one by one: "Good . . . bad . . . bad . . . bad . . . good . . . bad." Through his eyes I began to discover that the obvious was not art. He instilled in me an appreciation for independence in my approach to the making of images. In the beginning I was puzzled by what he liked and disliked, for the drawings I considered good—realistic heads of women with curly hair—he disdained. He liked the ones that were free expressions of the unconscious. I had no idea what they meant.

Sometimes, after a long afternoon of painting, he would take me out to dinner. Often we went to a Sixth Avenue dump, but the elevated trains overhead sounded like music from the spheres, for I was with him. We were in harmony, whether in conversation or in silence. Except for the physical act, we were lovers.

Roché, who had known Marcel for years, thought it wonderful that I had this opportunity to work with him and encouraged me to go to his studio as often as possible. He even teased me about being in love with Marcel. Instead of being jealous, he was delighted when I told him I dreamt of Marcel. For Roché loved Marcel too, as I think everyone who knew him did. Marcel was a beautiful, abstract, yet loving human being.

Henri, Marcel, and I often dined together, and both men would scold me about my lack of taste. They loved me in a paternal sort of way. Actually, they only wanted to cure me of my naïve idealism and bring me closer to reality. The two of them agreed about everything concerning me and conspired to see that my education took the course they approved. They were not interested in the theatre; they wanted me to concentrate on art. The three of us were something like *un amour a trois*; it was a divine experience in friendship.

The Arensberg Circle

One night Marcel took me to meet two of his close friends, Walter and Louise Arensberg, who lived several floors below him on West 67th Street.

The Arensbergs were collectors—the first in America to respond to modern art. Their large two-story duplex had a sitting room full of oriental rugs, carefully chosen early American furniture, and comfortable sofas and chairs. But there on the walls—not only in the sitting room, but in the hall, bedroom, bath, and kitchen—hung the most hideous collection of paintings I had ever seen.

Walking into this incredible home I caught my breath, suppressed a giggle, and sat down in a state of shock. One by one I confronted each disconcerting image as it shrieked out at me. The most awful, if I had to choose, was a Matisse, an outlandish woman with white streaks—like daggers—surrounding her entire body. Near the balcony was a Picasso filled with broken planes supposedly depicting a woman, and a Rousseau with a horrible dwarf in an unnatural landscape. Marcel's *Nude Descending a Staircase*—a wild bedlam of exploding shingles, as it had been called—had the place of honor. With great pride they pointed it out to me. I mumbled that it "seemed to move," praying they would let me get by with that comment. Nearby on a pedestal was a Brancusi brass that shot up in the air out of nowhere and made me uncomfortable. Scattered throughout the room were works by Picabia, Gleizes, Braque, and Sheeler, African carvings, and pieces from a mixture of periods. It made my head spin in disbelief.

Walter and Louise gave me such a warm and affectionate welcome that I felt at ease in spite of the paintings. The entire evening Marcel sat comfortably in a chair and observed my reactions. I had already told him that his Readymades were beyond me. He would answer with one of his favorite expressions: "*Cela n'a pas d'importance*,"—it doesn't matter.

Despite my absolute lack of true appreciation, the Arensbergs graciously insisted I come back often and, of course, I did.

Once again my life changed. At the Arensberg home I met poets, writers, painters, and actors. Night after night they gathered around the grand piano and carried on fascinating and knowledgeable discussions on every imaginable subject. All of the artists of New York were found there sooner or later—Marcel, Roché, Albert Gleizes, Jean Crotti and his wife Yvonne Chastel, Man Ray, Francis Picabia and his wife Gabrielle Buffet, John Covert, Walter Pach, Joseph Stella, and Charles Sheeler . . . holding forth on freedom of expression in art. Louise—otherwise known as Lou—and I would generally sit apart on the sofa, somewhat neglected by the others. She was not a beautiful woman; her nose was short and upturned, with lines on either side that ran down to her chin like streams

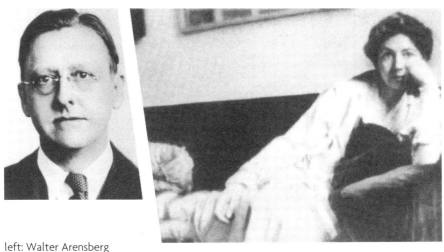

left: Walter Arensberg

right: Louise Arensberg was not a beautiful woman, but she was sincere and direct, and it gave her great charm.

trying to find a river. Her brown and curly hair was not flattering to her face. But she was direct and sincere, and it gave her great charm. Walter, a poet from Harvard, was also charming, but he was not quite so sincere. His cordiality lit up for callers. Like royalty, he was always the gracious host. Men liked his intellect, while women responded to his warmth like moths to light. Lou watched in silence. She knew that he was somewhat unrealistic, and it was upon her simple strength that he truly relied.

Roché and I visited the Arensbergs once or twice a week; Marcel would join us later on in the evening. All the while they would toy with me, mischievously teaching me bawdy French slang without explaining the meaning, then suppress their glee when I innocently used one of the words in conversation. One Russian intellect was so dismayed at my language he got down on his knees and begged me never to say such things again!

At midnight, Lou served drinks and hot chocolate, pastries and eclairs, and we would break up around one or two in the morning. As I listened to such inspired conversations, I often wondered what everyone was talking about, especially in the area of art. But I decided that since these beloved people thought the paintings had merit, and the artists whom they entertained spoke about them in hushed voices, the least I could do was try to enter their world of understanding. One night, while Sheeler and Stella discussed color theory, I gazed at the terrifying Matisse over the fireplace. It was his *Portrait of Mademoiselle Yvonne Landsberg*. Willing myself to be open-minded, I almost went into a trance. My eyes locked on its angular lines, until suddenly out of the canvas appeared a creature of wondrous beauty; Matisse had spoken, and at last, I listened.

The Arensberg's large two-story duplex had a sitting room full of oriental rugs, carefully chosen early American furniture, and comfortable sofas and chairs. But when I first saw their art collection, I thought it was an assembly of the most hideous things I had ever seen.

Meanwhile, Walter had become interested in the roles I was playing in the theatre and spent hours coaching me. Many evenings we left the others and went into his study, where I would practice my delivery. He loved the cadences of Shakespeare, and with infinite patience corrected my intonations. We worked on Marlowe's *Hero and Leander* and Mallarme's *L'Apres-midi d'un Faun*, first in French, then in Walter's English translation. I was fascinated by the uncompromising time he gave to details. However, I was losing my interest in the theatre. The stage, with its lustful directors, was growing unbearable. These exciting evenings with the Arensbergs were turning me away from the exhibitionism of the theatre to the subtler esthetics of the other arts.

For the next two years I led a magical existence. The Arensbergs brought me the culture of the day; Marcel had revived my interest in painting, and Roché was teaching me the depths of a love relationship. To have such a life after my stifled youth was incredible! My only unhappiness was the war waging in my beloved France, for which my American associates had little interest. In those days there were no televisions or cross-Atlantic airplanes. Even at the Arensbergs the war was never discussed; the only battles that occupied us were the ones against traditional values.

The members of the Arensberg circle were not content to be merely a salon of impassioned intellectuals. One day, after months of complaining about the restrictions of formal jury-selected art exhibitions, they decided to hold an exhibition in which anyone could exhibit simply by sending in six dollars. At that time juries were the *betes noires* of the art world. The experiment, to be called the First Exhibition of the Society of Independent Artists, was to take place in the huge Grand Central Palace. (This, incidentally, is not to be confused with the Armory show several years earlier.) Publicity was circulated inviting artists to submit their work, which would be presented without the tyranny of formal selection. Walter and Marcel, Walter Pach, and Picabia were the strongest forces behind the event; George Bellows, Walt Kuhn, Rockwell Kent, John Covert, Charles Sheeler, and Stella all helped with the bylaws. The poetess Mina Loy, as well as Arlene Dresser, Arthur Craven, and DeZayas joined in the activity.

Two days before the exhibition opened, there was a glistening white object in the storeroom getting readied to be put on the floor. I can remember Walter Arensberg and George Bellows standing in front of it, arguing. Bellows was facing Walter, his body on a menacing slant, his fists doubled, striking at the air in anger. Out of curiosity I approached.

"We cannot exhibit it," Bellows said hotly, taking out a handkerchief and wiping his forehead.

"We cannot refuse it, the entrance fee has been paid," gently answered Walter.

"It is indecent!" roared Bellows.

"That depends upon the point of view," added Walter, suppressing a grin. "Someone must have sent it as a joke. It is signed R. Mutt; sounds fishy to me," grumbled Bellows with disgust. Walter approached the object in question and touched its glossy surface. Then, with the dignity of a don addressing men at Harvard, he expounded: "A lovely form has been revealed, freed from its functional purpose, therefore a man clearly has made an aesthetic contribution."

The entry they were discussing was perched high on a wooden pedestal: a beautiful, white enamel oval form gleaming triumphantly on a black stand.

It was a man's urinal, turned on its back.

Bellows stepped away, then returned in rage as if he were going to pull it down. "We can't show it, that is all there is to it."

Walter lightly touched his arm, "This is what the whole exhibit is about; an opportunity to allow an artist to send in anything he chooses, for *the artist* to decide what is art, not someone else."

Bellows shook his arm away, protesting. "You mean to say, if a man sent in horse manure glued to a canvas that we would have to accept it!" "I'm afraid we would," said Walter, with a touch of undertaker's sadness. "If this is an artist's expression of beauty, we can do nothing but accept his choice." With diplomatic effort he pointed out, "If you can look at this entry objectively, you will see that

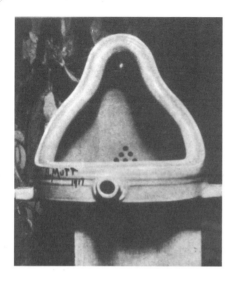

it has striking, sweeping lines. This Mr. Mutt has taken an ordinary object, placed it so that its useful significance disappears, and thus has created a new approach to the subject."

"It is gross, offensive! There is such a thing as decency."

The Blind Man editorial pages featuring Marcel's *Fountain*. Marcel's rejected urinal caused a small hurricane in art circles. I contributed the introductory comments to Louise Norton's editorial about the incident.

"Only in the eye of the beholder. You forget our bylaws."

R. Mutt, of course, was none other than Marcel testing the liberalism of the bylaws. He knew perfectly well that American puritanism would not allow total liberty of expression.

The *Fountain,* as it was called, was not shown.

Crowds of people came to see the exhibition. Marcel and Roché, intoxicated with its success, decided there should be a magazine published without editorial censorship. Mrs. Harry Payne Whitney, who had already started her museum and was sympathetic to artists, put up the money for its printing. Marcel, Roché, and I, like children, spent hours over the first issue, talking late into the night, pouring over the possibilities. The first issue of *The Blind Man,* as it was called, was something of a disappointment, but the second issue was another story. The rejection of R. Mutt's *Fountain* had caused a small hurricane of controversy in art circles and thus unfurled the banner of freedom in art. This gave Marcel an inspiration. We went to see noted photographer Alfred Stieglitz. At Marcel's request, he agreed to photograph the *Fountain* for the frontispiece of the magazine. He was greatly amused, but also felt it was important to fight bigotry in America. He took great pains with the lighting, and did it with such skill that a shadow fell across the urinal, suggesting a veil. The piece was renamed *Madonna of the Bathroom.*

The initials B.P.T. were featured on the cover of the second issue: P for Pierre, Roché's first name; B for Beatrice; and T for Totor, the pet name Roché and I called Marcel, although I had no idea why. Below the initials was a large picture of Marcel's *Broyeuse de Chocolat.* Stieglitz' photograph of the *Madonna* appeared on the front page with the heading, "Exhibit Refused by the Independents," and opposite was an editorial which I wrote:

"Whether Mr. Mutt with his own hands made the fountain or not has no importance. He CHOSE it. He took an ordinary article of life, placed it so that its useful significance disappeared under the new title and point of view, creating a new thought for that object."

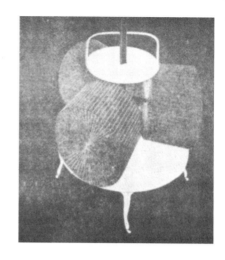

The Blind Man No. 2, May 1917, featuring Marcel's *Broyeuse de Chocolat*.

There followed an article entitled "Buddha of the Bathroom" by Louise Norton (who was then married to poet Allan Norton, but who would become the wife of Edgard Varèse). There were also two poems by Walter Arensberg, as well as a letter from Frank Crownenshield, editor of *Vanity Fair*:

Dear Blindman. You are, I hope, to be an instrument for the accomplishment of an important and much needed work in America; namely, the fostering and encouragement of a truly native art.

Stieglitz also sent in a letter:

This first exhibition is a concrete move in as I understand the Independent Society, its chief function is to smash antiquated academic ideas. This first exhibition is a concrete move in that direction . . . NO JURY . . . NO PRIZES . . . NO COMMERCIAL TRICKS.

There were also articles on Louis Michel Eilshemius, a primitive painter much championed by Marcel; poems by Demuth, Picabia, Mina Loy, and Frances Stevens; and a picture of Edgard Varèse by Clara Tice. To show our liberalism, we decided to print another point of view, so I wrote a stuffy letter from a mother, making a plea to keep the exhibition sane and beautiful:

"It is only by elevating the soul and keeping the eyes of our young filled with lovely images that we can expect good results from the generation that will follow. Cubists, futurists, are not artists. For Art is noble, and they are distorted, the line must be drawn somewhere."

We were out to save the world. We were young . . .

One afternoon, while Roché and Marcel were poring over the final proofs, they abruptly stopped when I arrived and motioned me to sit down. They had an urgent request: since they were both French citizens living in America, they hesitated putting their names on *The Blind Man* as publishers. Therefore, could they use my name? Delighted, I consented.

Mailing lists were assembled and plans made for the magazine to be distributed on newsstands and in the subways. All would have gone well except for my father. Although not the tyrant my mother was, he was understandably protective, and his views traditional and conservative. At three in the afternoon, on the day *The Blind Man* was to be released, I went home and discovered huge stacks of magazines piled high in our apartment entrance. My father came out of the sitting room to greet me. He had a strange expression on his face.

"It took two men to carry in these packages. I couldn't imagine what they were, so I opened one and saw they were magazines. I was astonished to find your name as publisher. You must be out of your mind. This is a filthy publication. I cannot believe a child of mine could be associated with such thoughts. I have never before interfered in your life, but I beg and plead with you to withdraw this from circulation." He continued sadly, without anger, "You are too young to understand the implications of what you are mixed up in. There are words in there no young girl should ever know. If it goes through the mail you will tangle with the law and be put in prison."

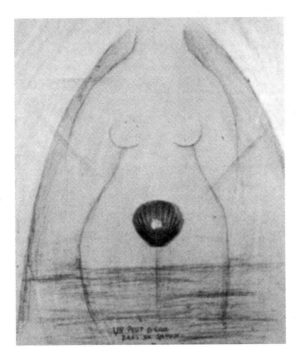

Un peu d'eau dans du savon
(A Little Water in Some Soap),
1977; replica of original work,
1917, destroyed.

The idea of jail did not bother me; it would be another new and exciting experience. But my father was a good and decent man, even if he did not understand art, poets, or painters. Moved by his despair, I raced down to see Frank Crownenshield at his office at *Vanity Fair*.

He received me with open arms, an amused grin on his face. He had pinched features and cheeks with little lines running all over his face like on a road map, but his eyes, small and alert, were dancing with enthusiasm.

Just the week before, we had gone over the proofs together and found nothing unprintable. But when I told him how my father had reacted, and suggested that other men might feel the same, Frank saw my point. Mrs. Whitney had put up the money and many prominent names, including Frank's, were associated with it. We had never thought about the laws concerning decency. What if our artistic tract was deemed pornographic? We dissolved into peals of laughter. "Your father must consider you the queen of anarchists," Frank chuckled. Although we still could not find the words my father objected to, Frank decided it would be best to bypass the mail and distribute *The Blind Man* by hand. This made our little issue a *succes du scandale*.

I ended up being involved in yet another scandal concerning the Grand Central Palace show. Marcel, with his whimsical humor, encouraged me to send two paintings to the exhibit. Of the many I had done at his studio, he chose a horrible composition called *Nuit Blanche*. Fifty years later, when it was hanging in the Philadelphia Museum of Art, I had a speck of understanding into why Marcel chose it. After all, what is taste? There is no true standard; people exposed to certain idioms of expression develop a sensitivity to their own personal values. I liked blue skies and Maxfield Parrish, but Marcel responded to works free of school influences.

In addition to *Nuit Blanche*, Marcel suggested that I send in an oil painting, a fairly abstract nude torso of a woman in a bathtub, shown from neck to knee with a piece of soap drawn at the "tactical" position. He studied the painting and said: "You must put a soap there, real soap, instead of painting it. Shop carefully and choose a piece that goes well in color and form with the composition."

He then helped me glue the scallop-shaped soap to the canvas, and when I mistakenly called the piece *Un peu d'eau dans du savon*, instead of *Un peu de savon dans l'eau*, he chose my slip of the tongue for its title—"a little water in soap."

To my astonishment, the painting, perhaps the first assemblage or abstraction by an American to be put on public view, attracted more attention than any other entry. Crowds stood in front of it chuckling, men left their calling cards, and the reviews gave it more space than that given to serious artists who truly deserved it. Marcel was delighted that his prankishness had come home to roost, and the harsh reviews pleased him all the more.

To celebrate the exhibition, a ball was planned to be held in Greenwich Village, and Marcel wanted me to make a poster for the event. This meant more happy hours in his studio. I sat on a stiff chair in the middle of the room and made sketch after sketch. When I was finished he took them and threw them on the floor. To my astonishment, he chose an insolent stick figure thumbing its nose at the world which I had tossed off. He took it to the printer, arranged for its size and color, and years later the poster became a highly treasured collector's item.

A costume ball was held in Greenwich Village in honor of *The Blindman* magazine. I drew an insolent stick figure thumbing its nose at the world for the poster advertising the event.

The Blindman's Ball was a riotous affair; the whole art world attended. Micho Ito, the famous Japanese dancer, gave an impressive performance, and I repeated my Russian folk dance. Marcel climbed up on a chandelier while the Arensbergs, Roché, and I applauded from a box. Joseph Stella had a duel over me, though I never found out why—something about protecting my honor, which no longer existed!

It was three in the morning when we gathered at the Arensbergs' apartment for scrambled eggs and wine. Since it was too late to go home, Mina Loy led several of us off to spend the night at Marcel's apartment. Sleepily, we threw ourselves onto his four-poster bed and closed our eyes like a collection of worn-out dolls. Mina took the bottom of the bed with Arlene Dresser against her, and Charles Demuth, the painter, lost no time in draping himself horizontally at right angles to the women, with one leg dangling to the floor, a trouser tugged up revealing a garter. Marcel, as host, took the least space and squeezed himself tight against the wall, while I tried to stretch out in the two inches left between him and the wall, an opportunity of discomfort that took me to heaven because I was so close to him. Lying practically on top of him, I could hear his beating heart and feel the coolness of his chest. Divinely happy, I never closed my eyes to sleep.

When I returned home, Mother was standing like an inquisitor at the door, ranting over my spending the night with Marcel. Her accusation went through me like a knife; she denounced me as if I were a harlot. All this for what she thought was my illicit night with a famous French artist. Imagine if she had known about Roché!

In tears, she complained that she never saw me anymore and had no idea how I spent my time. "I am twenty-two," I proclaimed. "You are always questioning me! From now on I will no longer tell you where I go nor what I do!" I saw her hands tremble while her next words revealed the dungeon in which she wanted to keep me. "I would rather see you dead than have a lover," she said, and buried her face in her hands.

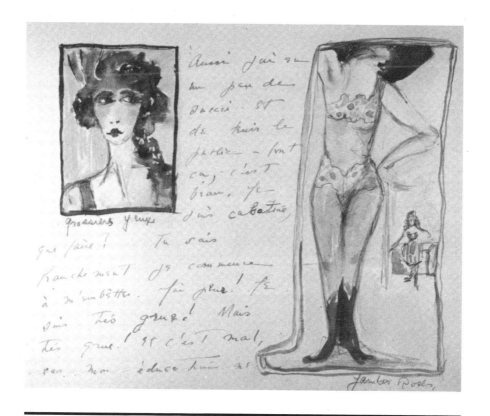

"... Also, I had some success at getting the attention of the audience ... I am a ham, what can I do? You know, frankly, I am beginning to bore myself. I am frightened! I am very abandoned ... and it's difficult because my education does not allow this [illicit love affair]."

—from *Pour Toi*, illustrated love letters to Henri-Pierre Roché, New York, 1918

"Now I am convinced virginity is stupid! One goes through life with the idea of virginity, instead of sleeping with men when they have the desire. The more we exist outside the system, the more creative we are."

—from *Pour Toi*

She loved me so much and believed I was a special, talented person who had to be protected. The last thing I wanted was her protection. Yet it was difficult for me to completely defy her, for I truly loved her. I was born willful and had an intensely independent, almost wild nature. She was ever the watchful hawk. We both suffered terribly, but perhaps my mother more, for she suffered the anguish only a mother can feel. She was a beautiful and generous woman, with great charm and style. Her friends loved her and thought me some kind of monster, which in a way I was. The real monster was the generation gap.

Roché and I were forever talking together. Even when we left off after hours of conversation, we could hardly wait to meet again.

Because I loved him so much, or perhaps because I was a woman, I wondered how many times he had been in love before he met me. I knew it was possible to love only once as we did. But he was forty years old. He had travelled and met many women. I decided since he was so old, he might have been in love twice before. Then, wanting to be generous and broad-minded about his past, I concluded he might have been in love three times. I did not want to hear about it, yet I did . . . One day I found the courage to ask.

He was resting on the couch near me, his arm around my shoulder. "Roché . . . you must have been in love before."

"Of course."

"Was it often?" I hoped he would say no.

"I don't remember."

"Oh, but you can't forget something like that."

"Cheri, a man doesn't think about how many times he's been in love." He kissed me.

"Please tell me," I snuggled up to him. "One does not forget when one sleeps with a person."

"It depends upon what you call love," he murmured, his arm tightening around me. "It's not always love when a man and woman sleep together. I have loved many women. I have forgotten how many. Perhaps a hundred, perhaps more. I do not even remember their names or what they looked like."

"A hundred! But that is awful!" I drew away from him, breathing like a tigress. "Falling in love isn't as easy as that."

He chuckled and drew me tight into his arms. "Men love easily. It is different with women. A man can sleep with a woman and never see her again."

"Oh, no!" I cried as my world shattered and my romantic dreams fell into pieces, never to be put back together. I could not conceive of being in the arms of a man without love.

He kissed me softly, his voice almost a whisper. "You see, had I met you earlier my ways would have been different. I would have loved you all my life. There would have been no other."

I felt faint. The world was not as I had imagined. I, who had chosen not to be protected from reality where love was concerned, now wanted very much to be protected.

Several weeks passed. Roché had to make a trip to Boston and I missed him terribly. When he returned he was more loving than ever, and we enjoyed being alone so much that we almost regretted the evenings spent with the Arensbergs.

One afternoon I went downtown shopping and found myself near his place. I phoned; he said I could come by for a short time, but that he was working on a government paper.

People in love are sensitive to each other. A few evenings later, it suddenly came over me that there was something different in the air.

"Roché?" I said.

A fly buzzed around the lamp.

"Yes." He continued typing.

The silence was wrong. I watched him.

Then I suddenly heard myself say: "You have been unfaithful to me."

He stopped typing and turned to me, sadness in his eyes.

"Yes."

"Oh . . ." I murmured.

"It was nothing. It did not mean a thing."

But I knew that it did. I saw the whole betrayal. "Alissa?" I whispered. My friend, Alissa.

"Yes."

He kissed my neck, my cheek; never had he been so tender. "Little one, believe me, it did not mean a thing. I do not love her. I was calling on her, talking about a book, the fire reflected on her white neck—and it happened."

Now I understood why she had been so eager for me to become friends with Varèse. Silently he held me, while the refrain kept going through my head, ". . . the fire reflected on her white neck." For the whiteness of a neck he threw away our relationship.

We both wept. At last I spoke, "I cannot understand . . . although I do understand . . . but it is so terrible for me that I cannot go on. This is the end between us."

His tears fell on my cheek, and mine on his. For an hour we remained in each other's arms, close as if we were one. I never suspected the world could be like this.

Finally I moved away from his embrace and, trembling inside, kissed him goodbye and walked out of his room.

With tears pouring down my face I took the subway and went home.

"You have been unfaithful to me."

The Lowest Point

In shock, I endured the next several weeks in a state of despair. Had I been older, more mature, I might have accepted Roché's infidelity—I do not know—instead, I felt I had been betrayed.

My relationship with Marcel soon took a more personal turn, now that I was no longer sleeping with his friend. It was natural that we would become as close physically as we were emotionally. It was a comfortable relationship, without agonizing ties or the tyranny of heartbreak.

One night he and Picabia took me to Coney Island. Because I feared roller coasters, they made me go on the most dangerous one over and over, until I could control my screams. They enjoyed themselves enormously. So did I, for with Marcel's arm around me I would have gone on any ride into hell with the same heroic abandon as Japanese lovers standing on the rim of volcanoes, ready to take the suicide leap.

It was late at night when we returned from Coney Island. Walking ahead of both men, I noticed three sailors coming toward me. A policeman saw them divide as I passed through and was about to arrest me for soliciting when Marcel came to my defense, while Picabia, who was Spanish, attacked the policeman with his fiery temper. To be mistaken for a prostitute crowned the dreamy evening, and we ended the night with roars of laughter. It was a respite from my depression and lingering unhappiness over Roché. Despite my love for Marcel, it was not the kind of romantic attachment that could cure a lover's heartache.

A theatrical agent approached me about going to Canada for three weeks to act in the French theatre in Montreal. I knew it would be helpful to get out of town for a short while. I also thought a trip to Canada might put some necessary distance between me and my mother.

When I told Mother I had accepted a job out of town, she forbade me to go. I retorted that my mind was made up. She threatened suicide, but I had heard that threat before. When she realized I was not going to change my mind, she went into such a fit of hysterics we had to get a nurse to put her to bed for two days.

While I was packing my father entered the room. "You are killing your mother."

"*She* is killing *me*. Since I am younger, *I* should have the chance to live."

I took the train to Montreal with fifteen dollars in my purse. I knew nothing about money and assumed everyone had ten thousand a year. Defiantly, I told my parents that money was not important. I soon found out otherwise.

The manager of the theatre met me at the station. When I told him I wanted an inexpensive room, he took me to a boarding house. I walked into a drab room

Marcel, Francis Picabia, and I at Coney Island, June 21, 1917.

with dingy curtains and no running water, only an old-fashioned washbowl with two skimpy towels hanging limply, as if they had given up the struggle. A worn cover lay on an old iron bed from which white paint was peeling, and two photographs of the king and queen of England hung on the wall. The slovenly landlady demanded the week's rent of seven dollars in advance, which left me with only eight dollars in my purse.

The room filled me with revulsion, yet I was the one who wanted to know about real life. Millions of people lived in rooms just like this one, and not by choice. I resolved to accept what I had bargained for. I took off my hat, sat down at a shaky table, and wrote my parents that I had arrived safely and would always let them know where I was. I put on a stamp, saw an ashtray filled with burnt cigarette remains, and broke down in sobs.

I went to bed, but was soon awakened by itching. Turning on the light, I found my pillow crawling with black bugs. The next morning I left, forsaking my rent, and walked to a decent hotel. Because I was in the French theatre and would get a paycheck in ten days I was extended credit. Put up in a clean, sunny room, I lived on crackers and bananas for three happy weeks.

When my contract with the theatre was up I planned to return to New York and look for another job, but my mother was writing me frantically, ordering me to come home. I realized her attitude remained unchanged. Even though the Canadian cold was shattering and the people in the theatre were vagabonds rather than actors, I decided to remain with them for the rest of the season.

The manager of the theatre was Belgian, a heavyset, broad-shouldered man who looked like a faded copy of Mussolini. His name was Paul, and he said he owned a canning factory, but he had the bearing of a gambler, not a gentleman. He neither read books nor cared for art; he had a passion for good food and talked about it most of the time. We had nothing in common, but I was so desperately lonely I started going to dinner with him. Mother's letters grew more demanding and Paul's invitations out were a comfort.

One day he suggested I move into his apartment "to save money." I thought it was time I became a woman of the world and someone's mistress, so with a certain recklessness I moved in. To my surprise he made no attempt to make love to me, although everyone in the theatre now thought we were lovers. This pleased me, as it labeled me a "bad woman" without my having to be one.

When I told Paul how my mother kept harassing me in her letters, he suggested: "Why don't you tell your mother that we are engaged. You don't have to marry me. I don't want to marry. Just tell her we are engaged and she will leave you alone."

He did not know my mother. She immediately announced the engagement to the New York papers. Although neither Paul nor I were seriously interested in being engaged, my mother wrote immediately, wanting to know the date of the wedding.

The last thing I had in mind was marriage. Paul was merely a welcome refuge from loneliness and the torment of my mother. I had affection for him, but we often quarreled because he was drinking, and his lack of taste annoyed me. In time I would have surely returned to New York, but mother put the fat in the fire. She came to Montreal and found out I was living in Paul's apartment. Confronting me, she revealed she had hired detectives to investigate Paul. They had discovered that he did not own a canning factory. Mother was adamant that I leave him at once and return with her to New York. I was distraught about Paul, who had befriended me and to whom I felt indebted.

Mother begged me to listen to her; Paul denied her vague charges. Finally, with indifference, he said, "Perhaps you had better marry me after all, and that will settle things with your mother. She will leave you alone."

Neither of us wanted to marry, but it seemed the best thing to do. Paul pointed out that, once married, my mother would have no authority over me and we could quickly have the ceremony annulled. We also agreed the marriage was in name only, with no intention on either side of having it consummated.

Terribly upset and confused, I asked, "Before we enter into anything legal, I want to know more about your past. Have you been married before? Have you any children, legal or illegitimate? I don't want to make anyone close to you unhappy."

"No," he grunted.

"Have you a mistress, any woman in your life who loves you, whom I might hurt?"

"No, no."

Annoyed, he assured me he was unencumbered and had no children. His parents were Catholic, his father was a notary to the king of Belgium, and his mother was a devout believer. Then he added that because I was not Catholic, he thought it wiser not to let his mother know about the marriage until later. I phoned Elizabeth Reynolds Hapgood and she suggested that we come to her house in Connecticut for the ceremony.

Paul and I took the train. I wore a dark blue dress with embroidered white flowers at the neck and wept all the way. The wedding took place two hours after we arrived. Elizabeth had arranged an altar covered with roses in her sitting room. I wore the same dress I had travelled in, perhaps as an insult to a marriage ceremony I really did not want. Though Paul spoke English fairly well, he was unable to repeat the words of the priest. His fumbling and stuttering all during the ceremony made me both giggle and weep.

After the wedding he and I went for a carriage drive together. I threw the wedding ring into a field. I had a dreadful headache; no bride could have been unhappier. After dinner I went upstairs to the room Elizabeth had provided. I found Paul under the covers, fast asleep. He snored throughout the night, neither knowing nor caring I was near.

We returned to Montreal the next day and checked into the Ritz. Wedding presents arrived, including checks from my family that amounted to three thousand dollars. I gave the money to Paul to deposit. Then we took an apartment and I read cookbooks, made ice cream, and was fairly happy to be left alone, playing the role of housewife. Paul still made no attempt to play the role of husband, in or out of the bedroom.

After three months, he suggested we move to New York. He chose a less expensive hotel and told me he was to earn $10,000 a year—doing what, I did not inquire. We went to the theatre, opera, good restaurants, and I introduced him to some of my friends. The Arensbergs were charming, as usual. I thought they would mind that Paul did not have a literary type of mind, but it did not seem to matter to them.

I dined with my parents twice a week, but we never spoke Paul's name, nor referred to what I was doing.

Paul liked expensive restaurants. The Beaux Arts was one of the best. One morning, after dining there on lobster and wine the night before, I said to him, "Today I want to buy that dress I told you about."

"Why not wait?" He whirled a glass of wine around in his hand.

"No, I must buy it now. It is on sale."

"I think you had better wait."

"I think I'd better not."

"No," he insisted.

"Why not?"

He hesitated, went to the window, and played with the tassels of his dressing gown. His pose resembled Rodin's statue of Balzac.

He took a sip of wine, then turned to me and said flatly, "You cannot buy the dress. I have decided."

I looked at him incredulously. "But you told me last week I could have it." He came and stood near me, smiling like a child. As if there were no way out, he blurted, "I have no money."

"What do you mean, you have no money?"

He smiled again apologetically and held open his hands. "I have only twenty-five cents."

The remark was preposterous. "How do you mean you have no money? What has happened?"

He continued to grin, "I had to send every cent to Canada. It is not serious, Coco."

I stood there in complete shock, wondering if I was hallucinating.

His face took on a dejected look. "I did not want you to worry, Coco. In three weeks I will have money from my factory. I just have to manage until then. A situation arose at the plant that took everything I had. I shall borrow a few hundred dollars and everything will be all right."

"You have business associates who will lend it to you?" I asked.

He hesitated, then said in a matter-of-fact tone, "No. You go to Walter Arensberg and ask him to lend me five hundred dollars."

"Impossible."

"But why not? He would be happy to help you."

"No . . . no, no!"

"But it is nothing. I'll pay it back in three weeks. Businessmen borrow all the time."

My father had brought me up to never borrow. I fought with Paul throughout the night; I explained that I loved the Arensbergs and wanted our friendship unsullied. No, no, I cannot borrow! Many painters had borrowed from them and not returned the money, and I could not become one of them.

I lay on the bed, my head hidden in the pillow, while in soothing tones he insisted, "It's only for three weeks. I will repay Walter one hundred dollars a week. I promise you, I give my word of honor. I will repay Walter beginning next week."

There are times when reason and feeling stop and the weight of the world makes a person numb. After twenty-four hours of Paul's pleading and haranguing, I was totally exhausted and gave in.

I went to Walter and borrowed five hundred dollars.

The first week Paul repaid one hundred dollars as promised. The same the second week, and again the third. Then he explained he needed five hundred more. Logically he pointed out how meticulously he had made the promised repayments of the last three weeks, and therefore he could be trusted. I went to

Walter and asked for another five hundred dollars. I felt like a hot iron was searing me.

Seven weeks passed and we continued seeing the Arensbergs, who never referred to the debt. One afternoon Lou took me to Maillard's for chocolate. Though it was hard bringing up the subject of the loan, now that it was almost paid back I said, "In another week all our debt will be taken care of. You do not know how horrible it has been for me to owe you money."

Surprised, Lou asked, "What do you mean the debt will be paid?"

"There is only one more week to go, thank heavens," I sighed with relief. "Paul told me he has paid you every week as promised."

"He has not. He has borrowed more. He now owes four thousand dollars!"

I burst into tears.

Lou saw that I knew nothing of the increased indebtedness and she tried to console me, saying it would probably be resolved. When I confronted Paul about the exorbitant debt, he brushed aside my concerns, saying that Walter understood his position and that there was nothing to worry about.

Paul never told any of us what the money was for, nor what he did with it. One thing was certain: He was not using it for our comfort. We had nothing to live on; the three-thousand-dollar wedding present was also long gone.

Above all I had to keep my parents ignorant of my situation, and never breathed a word about the loan to them. Soon we were forced to move out of the hotel to Greenwich Village, where rents were low. I took odd jobs: I modelled, packed gift parcels, helped a woman move, took in sewing, and accepted anything that would bring in some money.

Lost in Darkness

The next three years were ones of despair. The disgrace of owing money to my dearest friends was an ever-present weight on my shoulders.

Often Paul and I did not have even ten dollars, and I had no idea how to go about earning a living. I applied for jobs but my timid bearing got me nowhere. For someone like myself, who had always known plenty, poverty was crippling and left me in a trauma. One day on a bus, I noticed a woman opening her purse to pay the fare and it was full of dollars. I coveted the freedom this money represented, for I had none. I was on the fourth day of eating bean soup. My once casual remarks about the value of money haunted me daily.

I continued to visit my parents, dining with them twice a week. They asked no questions, I offered no information. They must have known I was hungry, for they made a point of having my favorite things at dinner. Once my mother's Chinese servant came in with a silver tray of food beautifully arranged and, to my dismay, was ordered to take it back to the kitchen because one potato was out of place.

Being without money began to affect my thinking. One day my mother asked me to go to her room and get a card from her purse. The purse was filled with money, and I actually contemplated stealing a few dollars. Having the thought, alone, was enough to make me feel like a thief. I wondered, are we good because we have never known temptation, or, having known it, resisted?

When Paul told me he was closing the factory, which by now I knew he never had, we were down to three dollars. For years I had collected fine art books and first editions, which I treasured. They meant nothing to Paul. He began with a beguiling grin, "Coco, I will have to sell some of your books."

Wearily, I gave him a first edition of Edna St. Vincent Millay and two beautiful volumes on modern art. He returned laden with food, a long loaf of bread, a ham, and pickles. Then he held out a jar and cooed like a dove. "Look Coco, I have brought you *marron glacees*!"

Marron glacees! He had taken my beloved books and with them bought imported sweets!

One day our landlady called.

"Beatrice," she asked, "Where is your rent?"

"Rent? Why I thought the rent was paid. I gave Paul some money to give you . . ."

"Beatrice," she said sternly, "it is your business to know whether or not your rent is paid. It is about time you came out of your dream world and faced reality. Some of us are pretty tired of your irresponsible attitude."

It was as if she had cut me in two.

Her words were truly one of the turning points of my life. From that time on I made it my business to see the rent was paid. I realized that being practical came before art, before anything, and that carrying one's own load was the first requirement of life.

With heavy heart, I redoubled my efforts to find work and walked the streets in discouragement. *Womens Wear* paid me ten dollars for an article. Morris Crawford was the editor—a dynamic man, and the first to draw attention to Peruvian textiles. I packed books for Robert Louis Stevenson's step-daughter, Mrs. Austin Strong, who told me I was the most negative person she had ever met. She gave me a lecture on positive thinking, but it did not help. She had enough to eat and was not married to Paul.

I felt I had touched the nadir of my existence. I knew I had to leave Paul, but my pity for him left me immobilized.

It was in this hopeless state that I read *Fortitude*, a story by Hugh Walpole. Like those devout souls who can at random insert a finger in the Bible and miraculously find exactly the solace they need to deliver them from the brink of desolation, I stumbled upon a passage in Walpole's story and clung to it, repeating it over and over. "Nothing that happens to a man from the outside is of importance; all that matters is the courage with which he goes through life." I repeated the phrase like a mantra, lulling myself into a different world of thought.

The following month, our landlady asked us to leave because we could not pay the rent. Elizabeth's mother offered me the use of her tiny apartment in Greenwich Village. Thankfully it was only large enough for one. Paul and I agreed that I would move in while he went to Canada to "check up on some new developments."

Just before Paul left for Canada, a lawyer with whom I had interviewed for a possible job asked me to join a party at the Hotel Astor. Four men and two women were in the smoke-filled room; one of the men had a narrow, elongated head, like a rat. His suit was grey striped, which made an interesting pattern as it rolled over his

The next three years were ones of despair.

belly. Someone whispered he had money and was spending a lot to get Harding elected president. He had his arm around a well-rounded blonde, whose figure was trying to get out of her dress. He left her to come and offer me a cocktail, which I refused, since I did not drink. I had always felt that if ever I was to be seduced I'd rather be sober. But the man pushed the drink on me, which I later tossed behind the radiator. He saw me do this and angrily assailed me for wasting good liquor!

Johnny, the lawyer, paid no attention to me until dinner was over, then asked me to go with him to his friend's room because he had forgotten a book there. Stepping out of the elevator I had a strange feeling. We walked down the long hotel corridor without saying a word and I had a curious tingling of excitement. When we entered the colorless room Johnny went to the window and drew the shade. I waited awkwardly in the middle of the room, wondering how to start a conversation. Then he came close to me and put his arms around me. I drew back, astonished by the abruptness of this attempt at intimacy.

His arms tightened and he soothed, "Don't be frightened, nothing is going to happen. You are all right."

Even if I had wanted to protest there was no time. Johnny pushed me onto the bed and draped my body with his. I closed my eyes. Shortly after "nothing is going to happen" was over he got up and that was that.

I was mortified, not for having slept with him, but for the way it had happened. I had broken the taboos of my youth. I had done what my mother had brought me up to abhor. I had been a loose woman. With Roché there had been love and affection. This was something else. At last there was a crack in the gilt that encased me. Curiously, in the degradation I found release, which is not something one would normally find under such circumstances. I felt alive, like another person. I was living my own life!

The next day I went to see Doctor Mary Halton, a gynecologist who took care of many literary and theatrical women. Edna St. Vincent Millay, one of her patients, told me about her. Bluntly I announced, "Yesterday I was immoral. Will you please see if I have a venereal disease. I want to protect others if I have." It had never occurred to me to worry before. Roché was a gentleman. Besides, it was a love affair.

She laughed. "It takes longer than a day for venereal disease to develop. Since you have come to see me, I will give you protection."

A marvelous woman, thin as a pencil, with black hair—probably dyed—and a sharp nose, Dr. Halton was one of the first to supply birth control to women. Every night she dressed formally and dined at the famous Brevoort Hotel, where the artists and literati gathered. She told me she saw so much misery during the day that the ritual helped to change the rhythm of her work. She felt women had a right to lead their own lives, and told patients if they knew of someone in trouble to bring her to the office, any time of the day or night. She protected

Johnny was the only human being with whom I had contact.

unmarried mothers. Edna, myself, and others put on a yearly ball to maintain a private room in one of the hospitals. Here Dr. Halton's patients could have privacy, for in those days an unmarried mother was put into a public ward, made to scrub floors to earn her keep, and was watched over by police who, after the baby was born, returned her to her hometown, whether she wanted to go or not.

Despite our rather unsavory beginning, Johnny and I met frequently during the next two years. He never said he loved me, nor told me anything about his life. Emotionally he never touched me, yet with my romantic nature I had to create love to endure it. We always met in the afternoon, usually at a friend's apartment. If he enjoyed my companionship he never mentioned it, but I enjoyed his. He was the only person with whom I had any contact. He made love to me like a rooster, and as dispassionately as if he were drinking a glass of water. It meant nothing to me; I lay there thinking of other things. But it did mean a great deal to me to be able to lie with my head on his shoulder. Just to have someone with whom I could talk was as comforting to me as a piece of driftwood to a drowning man.

Our backgrounds were from opposite poles. Johnny had earned his way since boyhood and had no formal education. But the quickness of his mind at thirty-eight made him a top lawyer in a big firm. He was unscrupulous, manipulating, with a nimbleness of wit that fascinated me. But he never manipulated me, nor I him. Had we loved each other it might have been different. He could have arranged jobs for me, but I refused to tell him I needed a job. I could not mention during one of our elaborate dinners that I had been eating soup for five days. I could not commercialize a relationship that kept me sane. Yet once, he did try to help, in his own way.

"I am in with the White House crowd," he said one day. "How would you like to be the official White House Mistress?"

I laughed and declined. He pressed its logic: "Jesse Wilson and Dougherty are close to Harding. We are sure Harding will be the next president, and they will be his right-hand men. Wilson would like a girl like you, well-read and educated. He would arrange it so you had no financial worries."

"Thank you, no."

My refusal did not penetrate. Four nights later, Johnny phoned, talking me into joining him at dinner. "Wilson will be there and I am on the spot, we are short a girl. He likes educated girls and I know he will like you." Six of us met at the Astor. Johnny put me next to Wilson and whispered, "Here is your chance." A heavyset peroxided blonde sat near, drinking heavily. I was sure she was a kept woman, the kind of person Johnny would have liked me to become. She glared at me: "Why aren't you drinking?"

Sharply I answered: "I don't make remarks about how much you drink, so kindly don't make remarks about how little I do."

Wilson, overhearing, leaned toward me and patted my back: "Good for you, girlie." A heavily built man, almost good looking, fifteen years earlier he might have been a handsome, clean cut boy. He was sweating in the brutal summer heat and did not impress me as being well-groomed in his perspiration-stained shirt.

Johnny, who had never been to my apartment, assumed that any place in Greenwich Village was a "joint."

"Why don't you show Mr. Wilson your Village apartment?" he whispered while the others were putting on their wraps. My refusal did not penetrate, and all of a sudden I found myself alone with this man while the others had slipped away.

He hailed a cab and I began wondering how I was going to handle this situation. We arrived at my apartment and he accompanied me upstairs, taking a great deal for granted.

The tiny apartment—a veritable love nest—was made for romantic encounters. Wilson plopped himself down on the sofa, the springs quaking as he did, and took off his coat. My heart beating fast, I moved as far away as I could get, which was not very far in a room that small. Not wanting to be rude, I said in the perfect hostess manner: "I will make you a cup of tea."

When I returned, Wilson put out his arms and pulled me to him. This time I had more experience at handling brief encounters. I gave a slight push, took hold of his hand, disengaged it, and said, in a voice full of regret, "I am terribly sorry to disappoint you. I do not know what John led you to expect, but it is out of the question."

Taken aback, Wilson sat down on the sofa, took a few sips of tea, then put on his coat and left. I could hear his footsteps beating a fast retreat down the stairs. Some time later, having become involved in the scandal that grew around the Harding administration, Wilson committed suicide. He was probably too fine a man to be associated with such corruption.

During the three months that Paul was in Montreal and I was living in Elizabeth's mother's apartment, there were many times when I wondered how I would exist through the week. It was at one such point that Marcel Duchamp, who I had not seen for some time, phoned and invited me to dinner.

We went to the Brevoort. We chatted happily and never discussed my marriage. Marcel told me he was teaching French for a living and playing chess as a hobby. After dinner we walked down to Washington Square to visit some of his friends, where a chess tournament was in full sway. On the way home, a block from my apartment, Marcel took an envelope from his pocket and pressed it into my hand. "Read this when you are alone in your room. Do not open it in front of anyone."

Amused, I laughed, "But we are alone now. What have you written that you cannot say to my face?"

He said hurriedly, "It is nothing, nothing at all, except you must read it when alone." Then he kissed me good night and walked quickly away.

What on earth had he written? Could it possibly be a proposal of marriage? Indeed, we were close enough at one time to have thought about it, but marriage did not hold much importance for either of us. I hurried up the stairs and breathlessly opened the envelope.

Inside was fifty dollars.

Marcel, hearing I was penniless, quietly, in his own way, made this loving gesture. Fifty dollars meant so much to me! Marcel's friendship and kindness, far more. Marcel was extremely astute about pictures, and his opinion was respected by everyone in the art world. Some thought his paintings so inventive that they were the most important contribution of this century, but for me the man overshadowed the artist. It was his humanity, his intelligence that saw beyond the immediate into the whole, that made him an individual of rare gentleness and integrity.

It was also during this time that I met the sculptor Constantin Brancusi. He was in New York for his first exhibition, and we struck up an immediate friendship. When we went shopping together he would choose the food carefully, like a peasant. Helen Freeman often joined us for dinner at my little apartment and Brancusi would entertain us with long tales full of fantasy and absurdity. There was one about a crocodile and log of wood I especially liked. One night I took him to meet the Arensbergs, for they had several of his pieces.

Roché was there. It was the first time we had seen each other since our sad parting. He had returned to Paris and was now back in New York on a visit. We were overjoyed to see one another. As always, he was intensely interested in my life and my painting. He insisted I needed the stimulation of someone near to release me from my banalities! Roché and I always remained friends, as people who have experienced true love often do.

My Affair with the Road

Since my financial straits showed no signs of improving, I decided to take a friend's advice and accept a part in a vaudeville sketch. Many leading actors went into vaudeville for short periods, as it was considered invaluable experience.

As leading lady, I played the part of a society woman who fought with her husband, then made up. There were others in the company: my stage husband— a mama's boy, who disliked having to kiss me in the scene—a comedian, and an ingenue with red hair and features that were easy to forget.

There were five people in the house for the first performance. In between shows, we spent the long hours in dingy, badly ventilated dressing rooms. For me it was an adventure, like going to a desert island where there were no utilities. Backstage held the same fascination for me as garrets did when I was painting. I enjoyed the crummy tables, cracked mirrors, and bad lighting. I suppose it was a reaction to the ornate period furniture with which I had been raised.

On the third day, the ingenue, a little frightened of me, asked, "You've been in vaudeville before?"

"No," I answered haughtily, "I was with the French theatre."

She began putting her red hair in curl papers. "I've been in vaudeville all my life and my parents before me."

I started to unhook my blue satin dress. In the mirror I saw her open her cold cream jar and start creaming her face. Her lips tightened as she put down the jar and she said, forcing the words, "You are letting down the act."

"How?"

"You are giving a mechanical performance."

"But there is no one in the house."

"That does not matter. If only one man is there and he has paid for his seat, he is entitled to the best that we can give him. Besides, in these out-of-the-way houses agents come to watch acts. One never knows when one is in the house. In vaudeville one is constantly watched. Every day, reports go back to headquarters. If you do not watch your pace, you endanger the living of the rest of us. Every preformance is the best. That is its tradition."

The value of opening in out-of-the-way dumps was that it allowed one to polish a role like clockwork. Every gesture—a nod of the head, a movement of the eyes—was worked upon until it was developed to perfection.

Once the act was perfected and we were on the road, the entire performance took fifteen minutes—but we had to give it twice or three times a day. It left the rest of the day for mischief. I was lonely. I had nothing in common with the actors, who called me "The Duchess" and left me to myself. The leading man, after his ordeal of kissing me, felt compelled to write letters to his mother, and the comedian was busy pursuing Patsy, the ingenue. Though they cuddled, I doubt it went any further.

I discovered that the old vaudeville people were really quite respectable. They did not know enough to be otherwise. They never read the newspaper, and the dressing room was their universe. Stuffily married teams concentrated only on their act, and nothing from the outside penetrated their little nest. Most of the acts were families who had travelled together for years. As far as I discerned they were completely without humor. It was only the short-term vaudeville perform-ers, like myself, who did not adhere to the traditional virtues of the old-timers and were willing to spend casual nights together. Not that I liked the idea, but recalling Marcel's objection to my sentimentality about sex, I decided it was time I behaved like other people.

There was an acrobat whose specialty was falling off tables. When he was not performing he wore thick-lensed glasses. The muscles on his neck stood out like ropes, though his skin was soft as silk. Deciding I had to stop being prudish, I spent a night with him. When he called me his "sweet cookie" while eating sausage with his knife, I decided I could learn about life elsewhere. I consoled myself with the thought that none of my friends could claim the dubious distinc-tion of having slept with a man who fell off tables for a living.

There was a juggler in Buffalo with a fox-like face, intense eyes, and a slightly pinched nose that pointed to the objects he threw in the air. He still had a touch of distinction, but a curious posture of vanity spoiled his otherwise strong features.

One night he invited me to supper. He told me he was a minister's son and had run away from home. He had spent years in the Orient and spoke several languages. Suddenly he brought back a nostalgia for the truly cultivated men and women I had known. Oh, God, I was attracted to him. What was I going to do?

"The world is changing," he said as he called the waiter, and I thought to myself how nice it would be to spend the night with him.

"One of these days the Orient is going to wake up, become industrialized," he went on, while I made bread crumbs with my fingers, thinking, "I wish he would ask me . . . yet I hope he won't . . ."

He amplified, ". . . the dancing girls of Arabia . . ."

Why did I hesitate with this man I liked? Because an instinct warned he might engulf me in directions I did not want? Strange Oriental practices or opium? His voice was soft, almost a whisper . . . "There is so much we could enjoy together. I do not want to urge you . . ." Why not? If only he urged, then I would not have to make the decision. All that was feminine about me longed for romantic companionship.

We talked until the restaurant closed, then walked down the street together.

The door of his hotel was in sight, mine was three blocks away. I slowed my walk, aware of his amusement at my struggle.

"You are an interesting and endearing woman," he said gently.

We were at the door of the hotel, both of us silent while fate waited for a decision. Then I heard myself say, "It must be good night . . . I have loved being with you." And I stumbled away into the dark night, walking quickly so that I would not change my mind.

This episode was a turning point in my life. I no longer wanted superficial encounters. I wanted love. No physical relation, without it, had any value for me. I was beginning to find myself.

To occupy myself I bought a typewriter, taught myself how to type, and began writing short stories about the vaudeville actors with whom I travelled. Each week there was a different group, and I focused my story on the performer who seemed most interesting. I cultivated these performers, making notes of what they said and did, and thus became friends with clowns, acrobats, jugglers, and singers.

I was especially fascinated by a group of acrobats. The mother, a matriarch, had a sewing machine, and spent all her off hours mending costumes, making dresses, cooking, and serving tea.

Another week there was a female impersonator on the bill. He was skinny and wore an evening gown, his muscles bulging. I saw no point in his being an impersonator, but he kept the audience laughing. A lovely actress in an apple-green tulle, with soft brown hair, came over, waiting for her cue. I liked her satin slippers and she told me where she bought them. On cue she ran to the stage and joined the impersonator in song. The act finished and the audience applauded loudly. The impersonator bowed, smiled, dashed into the wings, then ran back on stage and, with a swift gesture, pulled off his wig to show that he was a man. Because everyone knew it already they laughed even more. With applause mounting he reached for the girl and brought her to the center of the stage. Suddenly he grabbed her hair and pulled. Off it came. It too was a wig. Underneath was the cropped head of a man. "Hello, everybody," he said in a deep voice. The girl whose shoes I had admired was the real impersonator, while the skinny man was merely a decoy. It fooled everybody!

In another town there was a blonde singer, a girl with hair like Mayan gold and white skin like porcelain. She did not approve of the way I did makeup, which I had learned from French actresses. I could not convince her that my coloring was different from hers, and finally I allowed her to make me up. She took the hairpins from my long straight hair, curled it into a frizzle like hers, put black mascara on my deep-set eyes, and applied a dead white tone to my skin.

A well-known critic who was at the matinee came to her dressing room after the show and she asked him what he thought of me. "She may be a good actress," he replied, "But she was made up like a monkey and I could not take my eyes from the horrible mess on her face."

We were watched very closely from New York. One night the comedian, who had been hamming it up for weeks, outplayed himself. He fell into the sofa, touched the floor, and let his feet fly up in the air. Unable to control my mirth, I laughed in the middle of the fight staged with my husband, who also laughed, just for a moment. The next morning a telegram came: "What are you doing to the act?"

I never fell out of character again.

One morning at dawn, I was awakened by the sound of Patsy, the ingenue, and the comedian in the next room. She was sobbing, and I thought he might be trying to seduce her. I put the covers over my head and tried to sleep, but her sobbing continued.

Before long there was a knock at the door. I threw on my dressing gown and opened it. The comedian stood there, his face grave. I was angry and wondered what kind of excuses he had.

"Patsy's mother is dead. They phoned an hour ago." He collapsed in a chair and put his hand to his forehead. "Patsy is leaving in an hour for New York. Headquarters is sending in another ingenue. The act must go on. This is vaudeville." He shrugged his shoulders. "Meet me at the theatre for rehearsal at eleven."

The new ingenue, Sasha, was a slick chick from Brooklyn. Her hair was black, her eyes beady, and she strutted her good figure to constant advantage. With her arrival the tone of the play changed. She spoke the words, but without the spirit of the part. She considered herself the greatest actress of the stage and celebrated the fact by standing naked in the dressing room with the door open, her two breasts pointing for a millionaire. She walked around the wings in a loosely fitting gown, much of her falling out of it. Stage hands hated her and so did the actors.

Soon I decided I had enough of vaudeville and left the act to return to New York.

The Truth about Paul

I had not seen Paul for five months. I had no intention of resuming our "marriage," but somehow he managed to convince me that he had changed. He said that he needed me. Against my better judgment I consented to give him another chance, which meant moving back into a shoddy, third-class hotel in the theatrical district.

I had saved $550 from my work in vaudeville. It took Paul only a few days to extract it. He was as clever as ever, and I was as gullible and full of pity. The details of his "business" remained a mystery, as did the personal events of his past. He never introduced me to his friends, except for George, a man he had known when he was younger. George assumed I was Paul's mistress because I used my maiden name, and I was content to let him think so.

One warm night after dinner at an uptown cafe where George had invited us, we decided to walk down Broadway instead of taking a bus. Paul walked with the woman George had brought, while George and I walked ahead. Casually taking my arm, he said, "You are good for Paul. His wife was somber, a religionist. She prayed most of the time."

Even though I knew that I had heard correctly, I repeated, "His wife . . . oh, yes," and continued in an offhand manner. "She could not have been good for him . . . You said she *was* a religionist," I went on as if barely interested. "Did they divorce, or did she die?" Somehow I felt sure she had not died. In a flash I saw the whole sorry picture.

"Catholics cannot divorce. She is still living in Belgium."

We stopped at a shop window. As a point of distraction I began talking about Chinatown in San Francisco.

So Paul had a wife in Belgium; he was a bigamist. Now many things fell into place. I understood why he had not written his aged mother about our marriage, why he had stammered so at the ceremony. Given his twisted reasoning, he probably thought if he mumbled the marriage would not be valid.

I did not say a word to him that night as I lay in the twin bed near him. I wondered why he had suggested marriage in the first place, when there was no need for him to do so. It certainly was not for sex, for we had never consummated the union.

I was neither angry nor hurt. I was relieved. Now I knew that before long I would find the courage to leave him. I decided not to let him sense that I knew the truth. I would wait and let him betray himself. I needed legal evidence and he was clever at hiding everything.

Ten days passed. We were sitting at the window, and the street noises of a hot summer day were coming up from the sidewalk. I was reading; Paul was in

"I'm not married, I tell you."

his dressing gown, lolling in a chair.

Without warning he attacked, "George told you I was married."

"Yes."

"Well, I'm not!" he roared.

"Yes, you are," I replied, keeping my eyes on the book.

"I'm not. Aren't you going to believe what I tell you?"

"There is no use in carrying on like this," I said indifferently. "I know absolutely that you are married. I have no idea why you bother to deny it."

He walked up and down the room, swinging his arms like a madman, then came and stood formidably in front of me.

"What are you going to do?"

"I haven't the least idea. I will stay with you a little longer, but I will do something. I would help you, if only I knew how."

"Do anything you wish. I don't care. You're crazy, I have no wife in Belgium," he insisted, his eyes glowing like a wild beast. I was beyond fear.

I went to see Elizabeth, who once had been so happy to arrange our wedding. Words could not express how sorry I was for the way things had turned out. She was livid and wanted Paul put in jail. Legally he belonged there, but I would not hear of it. I wanted not only to protect him, but to keep the knowledge from his ancient mother.

Several days later I became ill. I could barely get out of bed. The muscles in my neck became so taut they went into muscular spasms. The tension was unbearable and even affected my thinking. For all these years I had carried the strain of my life in my back and neck, and now it had developed into an affliction. This was the beginning of a chronic and painful condition that I was fated to endure for the rest of my life.

One night, lying in bed in a pink nightgown with lace at the neck, my straight blonde hair falling to my shoulders, I glanced out at the street from the window of my third-class hotel room and listened to the tone of the city, the cry of the peddlers, the din of traffic, and the roar of elevated trains. My thoughts drifted back to the evenings spent with Marcel and the Arensbergs. Paul was in his bed reading *Variety*.

Listening to the noises in the kitchen, I thought I was in heaven.

I realized that I belonged with people who loved art and music. For four years I had done everything to help Paul. He was like a child moron who would never grow up. My pity would not help; he only dragged me down with him, every year to a lower level. I had to leave him or be destroyed.

Sitting upright against the pillows, I admitted that I had been postponing the inevitable ever since the marriage ceremony that was to have been annulled.

It was Wednesday night. I would leave him for good on Saturday. The next morning there was a great stillness inside me as I told him my decision.

A hurt expression came across his face. "Oh, Coco, you should not talk like this."

"This is the end. I am staying three days so that you can get used to the idea."

The next two nights with Paul were exhausting. He pleaded with me not to leave him, sobbing like a child. He blubbered that he would die if I left him alone. I held him close and told him over and over that I was leaving.

No decision had ever been so hard for me. It had taken years to find the courage to defy and leave my mother, but that was hardly comparable to leaving Paul. With Paul I was walking away from an emotionally retarded, helpless person, leaving him alone to face the world. All my maternal instincts were involved and I felt immeasurably sad.

I moved to a hotel five blocks away, where I had an inner room overlooking a brick wall. It was dark and noisy, but lying on the bed, staring out the window, listening to the racket from the kitchen, I thought I was in heaven.

I was alone; there was no one whom I felt I had an obligation to protect.

I could not, however, desert Paul altogether, and I continued to see him daily. When I told him the time had come to legally dissolve the marriage, he angrily insisted he was not married to anyone but me. I begged him to relent and give me the necessary information about his other marriage so that we could proceed with the annulment. He failed to understand that only my goodwill stood between him and prison. In the midst of my own legal problems, the Arensbergs' lawyer got in touch with me.

Evidently Walter had exhausted a fortune lending money, and now Lou insisted that if their marriage was to continue they would have to leave New York and start anew in California. The lawyer was putting their affairs in order, and therefore wanted to speak to me about Paul's debt. To my horror, I found out that Paul had borrowed more than nineteen thousand dollars, not including interest.

I could not understand how Walter had continued lending money to Paul without consulting me. But I knew Paul's gifts of persuasion all too well. To my further shock, I found out that Paul had pledged as security a ten-thousand-dollar legacy I was to receive from my grandmother. I protested, "My grandmother is still alive, and besides, the legacy is not even a certainty."

Heartsick, I went to see Walter and Lou. "If my grandmother dies before I do, of course I will hand over the legacy to you. But I am not sure she has left it to me. My father only once mentioned the possibility, and carelessly I mentioned it to Paul. My only wish is to pay you back every cent Paul has borrowed."

The lawyer, to protect the Arensbergs, went to see my father. Until then my parents knew nothing of this terrible and chronic dishonor. The lawyer wanted me to sign a chattel mortgage. But Elizabeth Hapgood and my parents insisted that I was not responsible for the debt beyond the first five hundred dollars. "I am responsible for all of it," I cried. "I introduced Paul to the Arensbergs. I will not let my friends be defrauded."

My mother, putting her hand on my arm, said, "You were not really married to that man. In no way are you legally responsible for his debts."

"It is not a question of legality," I continued, "It is one of moral responsibility. I am going to stand by the debt." They argued that Walter was also to blame, since he had known in the beginning that Paul borrowed the money without my knowledge.

When my parents saw how intractable I was, they decided I was a fool with no judgment. My father took me out of his will and left everything to my mother—which turned out to be an unfortunate mistake. By this time my parents knew the whole sad story about Paul and his wife in Belgium. They were wonderful, never reproached me, and only wanted to help me get out of the mess I was in.

When they learned that Paul would not cooperate in giving data, Mother decided that the only thing to do was for her to go to Europe and consult with his family. I wondered if deep down she realized I never would have married Paul if she had not put so much pressure on me when I went to Montreal.

Paul still could not accept the fact that I had left him. When we met he wept, begging me to come back. One day I accidentally ran into him in a crowded department store. He was overjoyed to see me. "Paul, won't you be sensible?" I gently implored. "My parents know about your marriage. If you won't help, my mother will go to Europe and see your mother. I certainly want to keep that from happening."

Violently agitated, he screamed: "I will kill her if she goes to my mother. I will kill all your family. What do they mean, behaving like this towards me? I tell you I am not married!"

I managed to get him out of the store to the sidewalk. Standing on the street with traffic roaring past, I pleaded: "Paul, just tell us the facts and give dates, then my mother will not have to go to Europe."

"Your family is crazy," he answered as his eyes narrowed. "If you come back and stay with me, all of this will be forgotten. I will forgive your family. Please come back and be near me."

He was irrational. My mother left for Europe and Paul became terrified that she would visit his mother. He accused my family of being crooks. I was astonished at the stubbornness with which he clung to the idea of his marriage with me.

One afternoon the phone rang; it was Paul shouting like a madman that he was on his way to kill me. He sounded crazy and I was frightened. I knew he was capable of violence—one evening when a gentleman friend saw me home Paul spit on us from the second-story window. Then, when I entered the room Paul grabbed me and pushed me against the wall, his fists clenched. I stood there, my arms limp at my side, and stared calmly at him.

I quickly wrote a note and slipped it under a blotter on my desk, with just the edge showing. It read, "If I am killed, Paul has done it." Then I sat down with a book and tried to calm my wildly beating heart.

The telephone rang. It was a friend, a man I had not seen for some time.

"Hurry, please come, Paul is on his way to see me and he says he is going to kill me," I shouted.

Putting down the phone, I heard heavy footsteps hurrying up the stairs. This was followed by a ponderous knocking at the door.

I opened the door quietly and said, "Come in."

Paul entered like a charging buffalo and leaned against the wall, his eyes gleaming.

"What is your mother doing in Europe?" He shouted in a voice I hardly recognized.

"Travelling."

"Has she been to see my family?"

"I do not know."

His face had turned purple. He pounded on the walls, screaming: "I am going to kill you!"

"All right," I said, unmoved, "but an old friend is on his way here. He will arrive any minute."

He leaned forward and studied me suspiciously, then muttered, "And you cheat me besides." How he could twist the truth.

There was such hurt in his eyes, I almost wept to look at him. He gasped, "You have ruined my life."

He turned to the wall and pounded it. My friend knocked on the door and I quickly opened it. He entered, smiled at Paul, and held out his hand.

Refusing the hand, Paul gaped at me, struggled for breath, and without a word turned and ran down the stairs. I did not see him again for weeks.

In Belgium, my mother had a long and satisfactory talk with Paul's parents. She not only met his wife, but also his little boy. The meeting between Mother and Paul's family was handled with gravity, but without bitterness. All necessary legal papers and affidavits were signed.

We started annulment proceedings as soon as she returned to America. We waited with other people at the court for our turn. I was nervous, because the judge, bored and irritable, slumped on his elbow, was hardly listening to what was being said. Our papers were in perfect order. Not only was Paul a bigamist, but the marriage had never been consummated. It took only fifteen minutes for the court to dissolve the marriage that had lasted four miserable years. I know my parents must have been as relieved as I. Had it not been for my mother's persistent and loving efforts, I might never have untangled this sad chapter in my life. Nothing, however, could ever undo the heartache I felt over the Arensbergs. We never mentioned Paul's name again, and it was years before I could talk about him, even to close friends.

The day after the annulment I met Paul. I told him our marriage was legally dissolved and that my mother had met his wife and son. I thought his eyes would bulge out of his head. He looked at me bewildered, like an animal caught in a trap, and walked away in silence. I watched him disappear amidst the crowds. I never heard from him again and have no idea what ever became of him.

Beatrice Wood, illustration for "Touching Certain Things," 1930

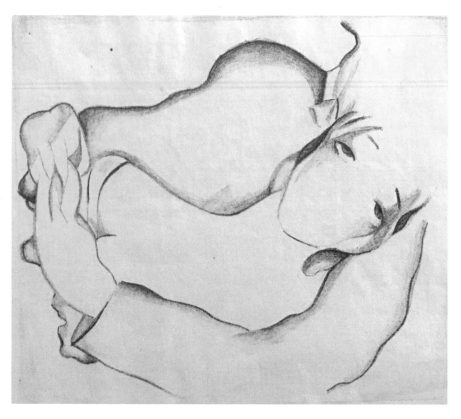

Beatrice Wood, Untitled Print, date unknown

PART TWO

Detail, *The Throne of Beato 102*. Mosaic installation created using
Beatrice Wood's works by Gail Cottman for the artist's 102nd birthday.

Another Great Love Comes into My Life

Reginald Pole

While I was still in the legal throes of ending my marriage, Helen Freeman asked me to act in a play she had written. She was to have the lead and I two small parts. She told me that a wonderful director was coming especially from California to help with the production. His name was Reginald Pole.

He was a tall Englishman with a lean face and grey eyes full of twinkle. If his nose had been larger, he would have resembled Abraham Lincoln. His tweeds accentuated his bony structure and gave him an appealing male sharpness. He had been born in the Orient, where his parents were missionaries, and had gone to Christ College at Cambridge at the same time as Rupert Brooke, with whom he had founded the Marlowe Society. Altogether charming and so-phisticated, when his glance met mine I felt myself sigh like a cricket singing to the moon.

Helen's play was not a success and closed after a week. But it did not matter, for the wheels of romance had been set in motion. Reginald and I began seeing each other fairly regularly. We met for dinner, staying long hours in restaurants, engrossed in conversation. Somehow he sensed I had earlier experienced a strange relationship and one evening asked me about it; I told him the whole miserable story. He was horrified. "I knew something was wrong," he said. "You walk as if you're carrying the weight of the world on your shoulders." I felt I was.

It was at this time that I began a serious search for answers to my deep, unresolved questions. Why was there so much violence in the human soul? I saw nothing but darkness and was suffocating in despair. Was courage all that mattered, as Hugh Walpole had written? Why did we have to go through so much pain and suffering? In quest of a solution, I asked my friends for books on religion and philosophy.

I read some Christian Science literature, but it seemed to deny the matter which it served. Nor did I respond to books that turned truth into a formula, or lulled the mind with mantras, or gave lessons on what to think. At the library I found a book by Babbitt which said colors had vibrations that affected people emotionally. "There is no reason why thought should not have form," Reginald commented. "We speak of anger as red, melancholy as blue, happiness as light, despair as dark. There must be electrical vibrations around individuals and colors which affect moods. There are some musicians who hear notes at a higher pitch than others." I was intrigued, but it was several more weeks before I found the information I was seeking.

Reginald and I were browsing in a bookstore, and I found two volumes by the theosophists Dr. Annie Besant and Charles Leadbeater, *Thought Forms* and *Man's Invisible Bodies*. We read them aloud to each other in great excitement, Reginald reciting in his deep, melodious voice.

Dr. Annie Besant was one of the most remarkable women of her day. George Bernard Shaw, in his unpublished diary, said she was the greatest woman orator of the century. An advocate of social causes and a benefactress, she was an influential crusader in both England and India.

I studied photographs of Annie Besant. She had a beautiful face and eyes of great purity. I wanted to find out more about her. "I remember hearing her name when I was in England," said Reginald. "She is a remarkable and courageous woman who did a lot for the working girl. She has gone to India and is helping with its fight for freedom. She used to be a free thinker. I did not know she believed in reincarnation."

"Do you believe in it?"

"Probably, since we obviously knew each other when we met."

I was elated. "You really think we knew each other before?"

He grinned. "You were probably a dancing girl in the Renaissance."

"No, I was your wife! How dare you refer to me as just an episode!"

He leaned over, put his hand on my arm, lifted my chin, and said with emotion: "Since when have you concluded men do not love their dancing girls?"

I relaxed.

A few days later we came to the Philosopher's Bookshop, run by Russell Jones. We bought everything we could find on Eastern thought, clairvoyance, and Theosophy. We were enthralled by what we read. Reginald remarked: "Theosophy started under great adepts—teachers who stressed the ideal of universal brotherhood, embracing a knowledge of the universe far beyond the scope of science."

I was now thirty years old.

Our evenings were enriched by discussions on Buddhism, Brahmanism, telepathy, and trance-mediumship. Later that year Reginald and I both joined the Theosophical Society. Dedicated to the study of world religion and occult sciences, it was founded in 1895, by Madam Helene Petrovna Blavatsky, an extraordinary and noble Russian woman who had spent years in India with some of the adepts, her mission being to transmit the great wisdom of the East to the West. After years of occult training by Masters of the Himalayan Brotherhood, she was sent into the outer world to assist humanity in its spiritual evolution. In *Secret Doctrine*—a volume still discussed by scientists today—she wrote of the creation of the solar system and the stages of universal evolution.

My parents hoped that I would return home after the annulment, but I had fallen in love with Reginald and knew I must keep away from my mother's watchful eye. I was now thirty years old. Reginald was giving lectures on art, literature, and philosophy at Harvard and Yale. Though he showed great interest in my company, there was nothing romantic in his conduct. On the contrary, he was quite impersonal.

One day he suggested we have dinner in Newark, where he was lecturing. After dinner he said, "I know it's late, but would you like to take a walk before you return to New York?"

A walk was not what I had in mind. "It is not late," I said. "I can start back any time."

He observed me with amused eyes. My heart stood still. Didn't he realize that this was a perfect opportunity for us to be truly together?

"But if we take a walk, it *will* be too late for you to go back alone to New York . . ." The question hung in the air. I lowered my head, then raised it and smiled. He smiled back. Still there was a silence. Finally, I managed to ask, "Do I have to go back?"

"No . . . no."

I held my breath as we entered his hotel. I saw him go to the clerk and write something in the register. When he came back, he said in a matter-of-fact voice, "Why don't you come upstairs and rest a bit."

I stood silently in the room as he went to the window and pulled down the shade. He returned to where I was standing and we shared a delicious moment full of anticipation. Then, in a low voice, I said, "I have a toothbrush and hair comb with me."

He laughed and put his arm around me. He had never touched me before. "You are a naughty girl," he murmured, kissing my neck, my head, my mouth. *A naughty girl*. Little did he know, I thought. Later, as we lay in bed, he asked, "And how did you happen to bring a toothbrush and comb?" I nestled against him shyly. "Perhaps I am a mind reader."

"No," he said thoughtfully, "You are a realist."

Four months of incredible happiness followed. We met every day and went away on trips over the weekends. There was a continual flow of ideas between us; the surroundings fell away and laughter and conversations swept us through time and space to a land of communion. We were so much in tune that our communication was almost telepathic. We read books together and went to the theatre and concerts, or to see friends. We acted like a married couple, although Reginald wanted to remain single. He was only recently separated from a wife in California and had a young son, Rupert, whom he adored. He insisted I was his wife in front of God, but I said I did not care. In truth, I was so in love with him that I longed for us to be married—I, who always insisted marriage was a nuisance. The walls of Jericho were crumbling down, but I kept this to myself.

Reginald decided to put on a special performance of Dostoevsky's *The Idiot*, and engaged Estelle Winwood, one of the finest actresses of the day, to play the lead opposite him. She was an "older" woman of forty-five, and experienced with men. Reginald was drawn to her, although he explained that it was only her mind that appealed to him. Reginald also found excuses to visit Tallulah Bankhead—another gifted actress who lived in the same hotel.

Reginald was not a good administrator, and the rehearsals went on with a great deal of confusion. A woman who had offered two thousand dollars to finance the production kept delaying the check and Reginald considered himself too much of a gentleman to press her. After waiting as long as he dared, Reginald suggested *I* confront her.

I faced the plump woman in her office. "The play is almost ready," I began. "The actors have been working for weeks."

Reginald loved to roam the streets until two or three in the morning.

"Yes, I understand Mr. Pole is a magnificent director," she gushed, as her bulging eyes moistened.

"The theatre is hired; the scenery will be delivered as soon as we have your check."

She made slight waves in the air with a lace handkerchief. "And Miss Winwood is such an able actress."

"Madame," I broke in, "you have guaranteed two thousand dollars for the production. We need your check. We cannot continue without it."

"Yes, of course. I will send it."

"No, Madame," I persevered. "You will either give that check as you promised, or we will conclude that you do not intend to do so and we will cancel the play." With that she opened a drawer, wrote a check for the amount, and handed it to me.

I wished that I had the same kind of successful forthrightness in my personal matters.

When Estelle Winwood heard what I had accomplished, she suggested that Reginald make me stage manager. I would do anything for Reginald, and he certainly needed help with the details of the production. I saw to it that the actors came in on cue, started the music on time, and rang down the curtains. I might have enjoyed the responsibility, except that at every rehearsal and performance I had to stand watching Reginald and Estelle in a torrid love scene. Fortunately, their impassioned embrace came at the end of the act and I had the satisfaction of bringing down the curtain with a bang.

The Idiot was a great success. Both Estelle and Reginald gave distinguished performances, and the critics wrote rave reviews. David Belasco, the most famous director of the day, came in person to congratulate Reginald. Belasco was an extraordinary showman. An eccentric dresser, he had white hair and wore a clergyman's collar. Other directors requested morning interviews with Reginald, but he declined, insisting that his asthma made it impossible for him to get up until noon. I noticed that he caught morning trains when he wanted to. However, he truly was a "late night personality" and loved to roam the streets until two or three in the morning. I, who loathed both getting in bed late and going for walks, went along with him as if I enjoyed it. My feminine philosophy dictated that a woman should do what a man wishes.

He especially enjoyed walking in dark, isolated places—until one night in Spicken Dival, an area of wooded terrain at the end of a subway run where criminals hid. We reached there at midnight one evening and headed straight into the most thickly wooded areas. I was scared to death.

We walked on until we reached a clearing; there was a full moon casting enchantment on the green knoll, our destination. Reginald remarked, "That path had a strange feeling."

"I thought so, too."

"Isn't it curious we both felt something unpleasant."

"I did not want to tell you before, but these woods are notorious for criminal assaults. There have been many murders here."

"That's just talk," he said as he put his arm around my shoulder and drew me to him. "Forget such nonsense."

The radiance of the moon lit up the vast sweep of woods and gave an eerie clarity to the place. I would have lost myself in this magic, except that behind us stretched that dark trail.

"When Wagner wrote Tristan . . ." Reginald began, already oblivious to the uneasy sensation we had both felt moments ago, ". . . he was trying to combine music and poetry. Beethoven, on the other hand, because of his deafness . . ." He went on, vaporizing about musicians, while I listened for sounds on the trail.

At the top of the hill there was a noise; faint at first, so that I was not sure I heard it, then louder. Footsteps were coming near.

"Reggie," I breathed softly. "Do not be alarmed, but there is someone coming down the path towards us."

We were both silent; then he too heard the steps.

I put my arm over his shoulder protectively. "Continue talking. Let us go on just as if we are not concerned, show no fear, and do not raise your voice louder than at present." He began again about Wagner and Beethoven.

Suddenly a dog ran up from behind and sniffed our feet; a man's voice came from the bushes, calling quietly to the dog. I decided it must be the Gamekeeper of Spicken Dival, who stalked lovers in the woods at night.

I held Reginald closer. "Music uplifts mankind," I said calmly. If we were to die our last words would concern art.

Reginald took up my thoughts. "Oriental music brings gifts using a different scale."

Footsteps came closer. The man was standing ten feet behind us. We waited. Complete silence. The minutes passed. Reginald and I began walking again. As we passed by the bush where the man was hidden, my heart fell to the bottom of my shoes, for he could have reached out and grabbed us both.

We climbed back up the trail still talking about music. Back to safety, I trembled like a leaf. Even Reginald was subdued by the experience. It put an end to our midnight walks in out-of-the-way places.

Several months passed; it was June 1923. Reginald and I were dining in a Chinese restaurant after an especially nice day. Toying with his chopsticks, there was a forced casualness in his voice. "You know, I think I should take a trip west and see my wife and son."

I swallowed and the chow mein lost its appeal. "I understood the separation from your wife was final." It sounded funny for him to refer to another woman as his wife. I could not understand why, when we were so happy together, he would think of returning to her for a visit.

I took a small apartment on 46th Street. Reginald went to his hotel only to check messages.

He put down his napkin, cleared his throat, and smiled at me indulgently. "I really should go see her. Of course, my best friend, Lloyd Wright, lives nearby, and if she needs advice she has him. But I would feel better if I went and saw her." Lloyd Wright was the son of the great architect, Frank Lloyd Wright, and an accomplished architect himself. I had met him the year before, when we were both attending a performance at the Provincetown Theatre.

Confused by Reginald's leaving, I clutched at the notion that he might be going back to arrange a divorce so that we could marry. I said nothing.

He took the train west, and for an unbearable two weeks I did not hear one word from him. Then he sent a letter saying that his wife had fallen in love with Lloyd Wright and they were going to be divorced. Soon I received a second letter telling me he was returning to New York.

My heart sang out.

He came back more devoted than ever, but he never mentioned marriage. I took a small apartment on 46th Street not far from the hotel where he lived. Instead of having to meet at restaurants or take long rides on subway trains, we finally had a place where we could sit and talk and spend nights together.

Reginald went to his hotel only to check for messages. It fooled nobody, but it gave him a proper front that kept people from asking questions. My little two-room apartment was up four flights of stairs, overlooking a court. It had no kitchen, only a sterno stove, and a card table for dining. One wall of the sitting room was lined with books and prints.

We created a wonderful life, reading to each other continually, going out, and talking endlessly. It was as close a relationship as Roché and I had enjoyed, except that Roché had been a teacher, beckoning me to come with him into the stream of life, helping me cross the currents, and always concentrating on my development. With Reginald neither of us was the teacher. Though his mind was burning with intellectual concepts, I challenged his philosophical flights and brought him down to earth. Sometimes we were more like two scholarly brothers instead of man and woman.

Reginald was musical and, while I was not, I pretended to be for him. During the hot weather, we often went to the outdoor stadium where William von Hoogstraten, director of the Philharmonic, was conducting. Reginald liked the way he interpreted Beethoven; I liked the set of his shoulders. A friend of my mother's who knew von Hoogstraten took me to a play where he arranged for me to meet him.

Knowing it would mean a great deal to Reginald to have an evening with such a noted conductor, I invited him to supper, explaining that a friend would join us later. Reginald at that time was rehearsing with John Barrymore, playing the ghost in *Hamlet*. Barrymore was not only famous for his profile, which threw women into a tizzy, but for his Hamlet, one of the best in theatrical history. It was the best, that is, when he was not drunk.

Von Hoogstraten and I enjoyed our supper, but Reginald failed to show up. It was late.

"Oh, but please wait another minute," I pleaded, "Reginald must be delayed at rehearsal. He wanted so much to meet you, and he will never forgive me if I let you go."

I made von Hoogstraten sit down and served him another bit of supper. We discussed plays, leading ladies, leading men, husbands, and lovers. It was midnight. No Reginald.

Finally it was one o'clock. I had by then exhausted every subject of conversation—not to mention both myself and my forbearing guest. Unhappily, I walked von Hoogstraten to the door. Just then came a soft, furtive knock. Then another soft, discreet knock. Von Hoogstraten's face was full of curiosity. I opened the door and there stood Reginald. Politely he said, "I have come to return a book."

The three of us burst into laughter; there was no way of escaping the truth of the situation. Reginald had simply forgotten. Now he was here to see me, feigning propriety. Von Hoogstraten

Seeing Reginald off

phoned the next day to see if I had time to "read the book," and whenever we met, he inquired with a twinkle in his eye about how I was progressing with "my reading."

Once again, for no apparent reason, in the midst of our happy days together, Reginald announced he was going to England to see his parents. I stopped breathing, not wanting to endure another separation. He went on as if talking to himself. "I have not seen them in years. My mother is getting old."

"Please don't stay long . . ." I murmured.

"I won't, dear, just a few weeks."

Rising abruptly, I went to the window and faced the dark silence of the night. I began to cry. He put an arm around me and whispered gently, "I love you and always will . . .," and buried his face in my hair.

Lawrence Tibbett—the opera singer—and I went to see Reginald off. Lawrence had been a student of Reginald's in California and Reginald, recognizing the quality of his voice, had urged him to come to New York to study. Lawrence was truly from the West; his father had been a sheriff. He was full of sunshine, open plains, and the earth. The three of us stood on the deck, talking until the last minute. The whistle blew. Reginald put his arms around me and held me as if he were afraid to let me go. I clung to him as if he might disappear forever. Then Lawrence pulled me away, and I stood forlornly on the pier, watching the boat getting smaller and smaller. I felt as if the blood was slowly draining from my body.

Lawrence Tibbett was asked to join the Metropolitan Opera.

Soon after that Lawrence came to see me with great excitement. "The Metropolitan Opera has asked me to join them," he said. "What do you think I should do?"

"Join, by all means!"

"But the salary is only fifty dollars a week and I may not even have a line to sing."

"You will have the prestige of the Metropolitan after your name. You want to be a concert singer. This will help you get bookings."

He put his hand to his head, troubled. "It is a grave decision. All my friends are out of town. You are the only one I can talk to."

Flattered that he wanted my advice, I sagely continued: "You have no name, no European training. I can't see what you could lose by joining."

"But they are putting me under contract."

"Join, I tell you. I have no doubt that soon you'll be given an opportunity to sing."

I was sure all his friends would have given him the same advice.

The opportunity came sooner than expected. Reginald had arrived back in New York and Lawrence's wife, Grace, came from California to join her husband on the East Coast. All of us felt Lawrence had reached a pinnacle of excellence when he sang in an opera starring the great Russian bass, Feodor Chaliapin, who Diaghilev had discovered. Several weeks later, the tenor playing opposite the famous Scotti became ill and Lawrence rushed in to replace him. The house went wild over this young American singer who, with no foreign training, gave a superb performance. My friends and I became a claque, not allowing the applause to die until our hands burned from clapping. The night was an historic event in musical circles.

Overnight Lawrence was the rage of New York. Soon his life changed. We saw him less and less. Grace Tibbett, a plain and unsophisticated woman who had slaved to support him while he was studying, was now deemed a handicap and Lawrence soon divorced her. He married a socialite and began drinking heavily. In a rather short time he lost his voice and destroyed his career. Fame is not meant for everyone.

At the end of winter, Reginald went to California to direct the annual Pilgrimage Play in Hollywood. He had been there only a few days when he wired for me to join him. This was to become a ritual we would carry out each spring for the next five years.

Joining Reginald in California I discovered—at first to my amusement—that he was very concerned about his reputation. As the director of a religious play about the life of Christ, he felt he had an image to protect. The new permissive society had not yet come. He wanted me with him all the time, but wanted no one else to know I existed. Once he insisted that I follow ten paces behind him as we walked down Hollywood Boulevard. I consented to play Indian princess for a while, although the deception was ridiculous. The fact that I laughed irreverently at his childish nonsense kept him on an even keel; he was a charming and distinguished man who everyone else took quite seriously.

The Arensbergs, who had moved to California in 1921, were delighted by my tales of Reginald's efforts to hide me from the Pilgrimage Players. Each visit to them I reported a new absurdity. They loved the story of the midnight ride Reginald and I took through the desert in his old Tin Lizzie. One night in the desert we stopped at a small group of houses, the largest of which had a sign: "Motel." Motels were an innovation then—there was no register to sign and no

Reginald playing the part of Judas in the annual Pilgrimage Play.

one cared who you were or what you did. Reginald asked for two rooms and a bath. The landlord measured us slowly and said, "You don't need two rooms."

In his best Shakespearean voice Reginald corrected, "We would like two separate rooms, far apart from each other."

The man caught my eye and winked. He gave us adjoining rooms, with a bath between. No sooner had the landlord's steps died away than Reginald went to his door and virtuously locked it.

Pretending fury I demanded, "Open that door!"

"I cannot," he exclaimed. "It is not proper."

I thought of the endless nights he stayed with me in New York, never caring whether it was proper or not. "Open that door," I repeated, "or I will scream and pretend you are attacking me."

Finally he opened the door but, hypocrite that he was, refused to sleep with me—although he managed to keep me up half the night with his snoring.

On another occasion, Reginald was forced to go to even greater extremes to protect our reputations. I was living on Shatto Place in Hollywood, opposite the Good Samaritan Hospital, in an apartment overseen by a formidable landlady. Directing the play was arduous for Reginald and he would arrive—rather I should say "sneak"—into my place very late at night. Often we stayed up until two or three in the morning and slept in. One particular morning, through my half-slumbering senses, I heard Reginald shouting from the bathroom. I opened my eyes to see him rushing into the room stark naked, followed by a torrent of water—the toilet had overflowed! The water poured into the room, turning the carpet into a sponge and threatening to ruin the floor. I threw Reginald his clothes, pushed him out of sight into the kitchen, and raced across the hall in my nightgown to get the landlady. She returned with me, nonchalantly reviewed the crisis with a glance, marched into the bathroom, turned off the valve, and stopped the water. Then she announced, "I'll get a mop from the kitchen."

My heart stood still. I opened my mouth to stop her, but no sound came out. Paralyzed, I watched her pass through the kitchen door, praying God would dissolve Reginald, or me.

She marched into the kitchen, slammed a closet door, then strode back out and began mopping without a word. Her silence puzzled me.

I tiptoed into the kitchen, looked around, and saw—no one. I searched behind the door of the broom closet, looked in the oven. Reginald was nowhere to be seen, yet there was no place for him to hide, nor time for him to disappear. Was I losing my mind?

Twenty minutes later the phone rang. It was Reginald. He whispered, "Are you alone?!"

"Where are you?!"

"Around the corner at the drugstore. I jumped out of the window as fast as I could, pulling up my zipper as I did so. It was the quickest military maneuver I have ever executed."

"Did the landlady see you?"

"No. I jumped as she opened the door, holding my pants up as I climbed out of the window!"

The window was twelve feet from the street—not so high as to be fatal, but high enough to make a half-dressed man hurrying out of it look ridiculous. I hoped the patients at the hospital across the street were entertained.

The Arensbergs complained that the windows of the Wright house were at the wrong height.

The Arensbergs loved this story. Without their art collection or the stimulation of their old friends, they were living a rather dull existence in a small bungalow on Whitley in Hollywood. Hollywood had a vitality of its own, but it did not offer the intellectual and artistic delights of New York. Walter was deep in pursuit of his Baconian theory. He believed Francis Bacon was the true author of the Shakespearean plays, and he worked late into the night deciphering cryptograms with which he hoped to prove his thesis.

The Whitley bungalow was a run-of-the-mill two-bedroom house which they preferred to the Frank Lloyd Wright house at Olive Hill in which they had been living. They complained that the windows of the Wright house, which Aline Barnsdall had commissioned, were at the wrong height and that the closets were too high. They were much happier in this small, ordinary bungalow. Lou did the cooking and they ate on a small table in the kitchen. The view from the kitchen window was of other bungalows. Often Lou would sit there eating an apple and cheese; she liked simple food. She wore cheap little bargain basement print dresses, and because she was as straight as the shingle of a house they looked stylish on her.

It was hard for me to believe that the famous host and hostess of the New York art crowd could really be happy here, just being together and attending the chores of daily existence. Walter started becoming so absentminded that once when Lou asked him if he wanted salad for lunch, he looked at her blankly and said, "Salad? What's salad?" We teased him mercilessly after that and "What's salad?" became our byline whenever he looked absentminded.

I Lose My Heart in the Desert

When the season for the Pilgrimage Play was over, Reginald and I started back east by train. He asked, "Wouldn't you like to see more of this beautiful country? We'll make one stop. You choose the town."

I studied the map and decided I liked the name Gallup, in New Mexico.

We meant to stay only a few hours, but when we learned that a ceremonial festival was taking place and that Native Americans from various tribes would be coming, we opted to stay the weekend.

We loved the clean air and the sound of the tribes chanting in the distance. I was transfigured, never having heard such music. It was elemental, like the earth breathing.

Hundreds of Native Americans were everywhere, wearing their finest costumes and jewelry. In the richness of ritual and dance, it was hard deciding which tribe was the most beautiful. But it was not difficult selecting the one man who was the most handsome. There was a young Santa Domingan who stood out among the rest.

The next morning, enchanted by the desert air and vibrant color of the sky, I went walking by myself to the outskirts of the town. As I came to the end of the street, I noticed a figure coming toward me. It was my attractive young Santa Domingan. He waved. I waved back. Then he ran up and held out his hand for me to take.

"You like ceremonial?"

"Yes!"

He pointed at the *wampum* around my neck. "You wear turquoise necklace. Necklace badly strung. You take off necklace. You give me. I have restrung."

We were alone, with no one else in sight. I had been told that these people love turquoise and were known to steal it. I took off the necklace, willing to lose it rather than mistrust such a magnificent creature.

"But I am taking the train in two hours," I said. "If you can get it restrung for me, bring it to the hotel. I am staying at . . ."

He interrupted. "I know. Small hotel. I bring back necklace before your train leaves. I know your name. I know all about you. I come help carry your bags to train."

I rushed back and told Reginald about my encounter.

He grinned indulgently. "You can kiss the necklace goodbye."

"How dare you," I gasped. "Of course he will bring it back. He has the most beautiful face."

In 1925, I took a trip to Gallup, New Mexico, with Reginald. I loved the land, but I lost my heart to a handsome Santa Domingan Indian named Patisco Quintano.

Reginald shook his head in despair. "You are the most trusting creature alive."

I began to talk rapidly. "He *will* bring it back. He is coming to the hotel to pick up my bags. He even knew where I was staying." I gave Reginald an exalted hug and continued: "Now, when he comes pretend that you don't know me, that you don't have anything to do with me. He is walking to the station with me and I want to be alone with him."

"Yes, all right," Reginald replied, amused: "I'll follow discreetly behind in case you need rescue. " He had made me walk behind him often enough!

I sighed rapturously, "I am going to be a squaw."

My Santa Domingan arrived, in time, and with the necklace restrung. He put it around my neck, picked up my grips, and began walking slowly with me toward the station. I took his picture, wrote down his name and address and the name of his friend, Sunshine Young Deer, to whom I was to send a copy of the picture.

After a few words he asked carefully, "You married?"

"No."

"Your father living?"

"Yes."

"Your mother living?" I nodded my head. "Your home New York? Big city?" "Yes."

There was a silence, while I was trying to make up my mind whether he was proposing, and if so, whether I should consider the adventure of sleeping in a teepee.

"You like me?" he asked gravely.

Just as I was about to reply, "Yes," the train whistle blew. Starting at the sound, I saw Reginald watching me from a distance, grinning.

There was no more time to talk to my new friend. He said emphatically, "You come back. You write. You no forget me."

Reginald and I boarded opposite ends of the car, Reginald leaning back from the steps to make sure I was on. I waved madly at the tall, dignified, expressionless figure of my admirer as the train moved out.

Soon the sandy dunes and purple hills of the desert took over. "Oh, Reggie," I signed wanly, "I wonder what it would be like hugging a man on a donkey, a papoose on my back? I should have gone off with him for a week."

Reginald's blue eyes twinkled as he said, "I think so, too."

I gave him a kick.

The adventure did not end there. Patisco Quintano, as my Native American friend was called, was well respected in his tribe, a man of honor and responsibility. Upon returning to New York, I began corresponding with him, as well as with Sunshine Young Deer. Patisco often asked me to buy bells and other items for his tribe, for which he paid by return mail.

Several months went by before I found out that Sunshine Young Deer was a woman, not a man. That took some of the zest out of our correspondence. She and her husband were in a vaudeville act, and I went to meet them when they came to New York. He was an acrobat and Sunshine did rope routines. "You heard from Patisco Quintano recently?" she asked when I visited her backstage.

"Yes," I answered proudly, "last week."

"He wrote me, too." I did not like that. "I also received a letter from him yesterday." Now I definitely felt betrayed.

"He writes you often?"

"Oh, yes," she said, dabbing cold cream over her face. "He writes me often. He is my daddy."

I did not want to intrude into her private life, but I was curious as to what she meant by "daddy."

"Your daddy . . .?" I asked. "Do you mean . . . 'sugar daddy?'"

A curious expression came over her face, as if she were controlling a smile. "No, he is my father."

"Impossible! He can't be over twenty-eight."

She laughed. "He is fifty-six. *I* am thirty-two." I was astonished. Later

Reginald condescendingly informed me that Native Americans always look much younger than their years.

The following summer Patisco invited me to spend a week with him and his people at the pueblo. It was a wonderful opportunity, and I looked forward to visiting him on my way out to see Reginald in California. But an unexpected flare-up of my neck problem forced me to delay the trip. Several days later, travelling west, I decided to stop in Gallup anyway. It was off season, pouring rain, and depressing. Sitting forlornly in the dreary hotel lobby, I suddenly recognized Minister of Indian Affairs John Collyer, whom I had once heard lecture. I introduced myself and I told him about my "love affair." He graciously invited me to join him and his two sons on a three-day tour of the Indian country, ending at Santa Domingo, where Patisco lived.

The next morning Collyer, his two sons, and I started out. We spent the night miles away from civilization, sleeping on the ground under Inscription Rock. The boys had been trained to break camp since childhood; they started a fire and assembled grasses for soft beds. I, who had never been away from a mattress in my life, snuggled into the fragrance of wild weeds. The next day we visited small pueblos and met craggy-faced chiefs with whom Collyer consulted.

On the last day—the day we were to arrive in Santa Domingo—I awoke with an excruciating headache. The long hours in the car and the glaring sun had caused the muscles in my neck to tighten; the ligaments were as hard as steel. I was too sick to raise my head and lay in the back seat of the car, nauseated and wanting to die.

We arrived at Patisco's pueblo and I dragged myself out of the car, dazed and ill. Walking unsteadily, I faced my friend with a miserable smile, while his darling, chubby wife greeted me, holding out a platter of lemons. I wanted so much to visit with them but was too ill even to speak. Knowing the stoicism of Native Americans, I was embarrassed to admit my discomfort, and ashamed that I could not overcome it.

It looked as if I was not meant to pursue my primitive love adventure after all, and I left the desert, never to return.

The Spirit and the Flesh

Back in New York, Reginald met Krishnamurti, the East Indian who Dr. Annie Besant had proclaimed to be a great world teacher. She and Charles Leadbeater, the Anglican priest with whom Dr. Besant worked and wrote, had been instructed to watch for a highly evolved person who would bring truth in new forms to the world. In Adyar, in Madras, India, Leadbeater, who was clairvoyant, noticed two young brothers at the water's edge. One of them, Jiddu Krishnamurti, had a particularly large aura. Both Dr. Besant and Leadbeater felt they had found the individual they sought and took charge of his education.

(Middle row, from left) Krishnamurti, Dr. Annie Besant, and Charles Leadbeater. (In front) Nytyananda.

Reginald immediately arranged for him to visit my place for lunch, but I was not in the habit of entertaining distinguished people, especially those of a spiritual bearing. "What shall I give him?" I cried, aghast.

"Salad. With thinly sliced raw potato," Reginald announced.

"That is not something to serve a guest!" Certainly it was some eccentric idea Reginald had gotten into his head, but he persevered.

"It is delicious. He will love it."

I was nervous about receiving Krishnamurti in my modest place, but his exquisite manners quickly put me at ease. He was in his late twenties, immaculately dressed, and had lustrous, brown eyes of extraordinary depth and heavy, dark hair. No wonder painters raved about his face.

He courteously held out a chair for me to sit down and exclaimed at the potato. "What is this?"

"Raw potato," answered Reginald proudly.

"Raw potato? That is one thing I have never had before," Krishnamurti said, chuckling, while I wanted to slip through the floor.

After luncheon the three of us went to the Metropolitan Museum of Art to visit the Oriental Collection. Reginald and Krishnamurti were absorbed in conversation about art and music while I followed silently like a good oriental wife who never speaks in front of her husband's guests.

Shortly afterward, I was invited to dinner with Krishnamurti, his brother Nytyananda, and his great friend, D. Rajagopal, next to whom I was seated.

I found Rajagopal enormously attractive, but was too timid to say a word. Nytyananda watched me and smiled with a beautiful understanding expression. Sadly, he died a year later, but I never forgot the warmth of his smile.

Krishnamurti had an electrical magnetism around him, and he seemed put together like a stainless steel spring.

I did not know it then, but my association with Krishnamurti and my attraction to his wisdom was to greatly influence my life and affect its course in the years to come.

My relationship with Reginald continued to be close; however, I was beginning to recognize certain flaws in his nature which I feared would keep him from ever realizing his potential. Once, for example, after Reginald gave a brilliant lecture on the mental process of discovery, a philanthropist, Maj. Phelps Stokes, had been so impressed he offered to finance its publication. Reginald was enthused, but weeks passed by before he wrote a line. I scolded, "You cannot possibly remember . . ."

"But I remember everything," he proclaimed, reassuring me with a disarming little peck on my cheek.

Two months passed. When he read me what he had finally written, nothing was left of the substance of the lecture.

"Darling, this is not your lecture," I cried, taking hold of his hand and trying to hide my disillusionment about his judgment.

"It is the essence of my lecture," he answered fiercely.

"No, no, no! Your lecture was inspiring. This is just a collection of sentences." I hesitated, then blurted out, determined that he face reality, "It is nothing but hot air."

Maj. Stokes was disappointed, and I began to perceive that my giant of wisdom was not always such a genius. I also noticed that he seemed to suffer attacks of asthma whenever he wanted to avoid something.

Although he loved to speak of creating spiritual links with me, he was forever romanticizing about falling in love with various damsels—like the lovestruck poet Shelley had done. Idle as this pursuit was, it bothered me enormously, and more so that he teased me about it. I was like Humpty Dumpty. Ever since Roché, my sense of security in love affairs was fragile.

"I cannot love a woman once I have touched her," he would spout. "Byron fell out of love with the woman who inspired him when he saw her eating."

"Rubbish," I answered. The night before, touching a woman had not bothered him in the least.

Back in California for the next play season, I discussed Reginald's lack of organization and his inability to sustain hard work with the Arensbergs. We admitted his talent, but were upset he did so little with it.

I feared the trouble was that he was beginning to over identify with the Biblical roles he was performing in the annual Pilgrimage Plays.

One day we were walking down Hollywood Boulevard when a woman approached him with prayerful hands, bowed her head, and said in a purring voice: "Jesus."

Reginald replied: "Yes?"

I teased the tar out of him forever after that. Whenever he got on a spiritual height I called out, "Jesus," in withering tones. He wanted to save the world, but looked down at it from great spiritual heights.

"If once you dropped your pseudo-intellectualism and allowed yourself to be a part of the world, to lust, your work would expand," I said vehemently. "Without the passion of emotion, nothing gets done. Don't play at being a phantom."

I feared the trouble was that he was beginning to overidentify with the biblical roles he was performing.

When he pretended not to hear I began to cry, and he came to put his arms gently around me.

"There, there," he soothed. "You and I will meditate. You are too emotional. Of course I love you, but I am detached and you must be detached. "

It was not long before he gave an example of his detachment.

I left him in California and went back early to New York to get the place in order for his return three weeks later. In New York, I dreamed Reginald was in love with someone else and awoke in tears. I dismissed the dream. A few days later the dream recurred. I wrote him about it, but he did not respond.

The dream came back a third time and my pillow was wet with tears. I wrote him and demanded an answer.

A telegram arrived. He was in love with a twenty-two-year-old poet and planned to marry her.

I was stupified. For some reason I wrote him a note sending my love and wishing them happiness. Then it was as if I died. I sat in a chair for two days, unable to speak or eat. For nights I lay in bed with my eyes wide open. How could this have happened? For six years Reginald convinced me that we were weaving ties that would hold forever. He told me I was his wife before God. Why do women believe men?

A week later he wired he was returning to New York to see me. I met him at the station and we stared at each other like strangers. He smiled wistfully and I smiled back sadly as we headed to my apartment. I could not imagine why he had returned. Once upstairs, I sat formally on the couch while he stood, studying me. "You look very pretty," he offered.

I did not answer.

"I could not bear to be without news of you," he announced solemnly. "I still love Leslyn. She loves me. We decided, however, that you need me more than she does."

My heart was thumping but I could not speak. He went on with forced objectivity.

"She feels very kindly about you . . ." A new woman can afford to feel generous toward the one who has been discarded.

"I told her how much I love you, how much you mean to my life. She is more detached than you, more emotionally controlled . . ."

And she is a poet, I thought.

"She is working for her college degree and agreed it would be wise for us to separate until she graduates."

"Then you plan to be in New York for a while?" I asked numbly. "Are you going to be at your old hotel?"

"Yes, but tonight I will sleep here."

With the heaviness of unexpected happiness, I moved to the window. He came and put his hands on my shoulders, turned me around, and held me away from him. Then we were in each other's arms, tenderly, without passion.

That night he slept with me, and every other night during winter, but in a purely platonic way, without any sexual intimacy. He wrote Leslyn daily and talked endlessly to me about her.

"Detachment, darling," I said to myself and pretended to read a magazine.

A friend had introduced Reginald to Maud Allen, a dancer nearly as famous as Isadora Duncan. When he told her about his idea of combining philosophical words with melody, she commissioned him to compose a one-act play in which she would dance and talk; the play was to be presented as part of a benefit performance at the Metropolitan Opera.

One evening, while we were sipping hot chocolate, he suddenly said, "Leslyn has been writing discouraging letters. She says she loves me, but is no longer in love with me."

"Oh."

"I can't bear it," he said. "I shall have to do something about it." He walked up and down the room.

He stopped and said, "I shall have to go west and see her. I shall have to hear her say 'no' to my face, or else I will always think that my absence has changed her."

He started again to pace. Annoyed at my silence, he pressed: "What do you think I should do? Please advise. Should I go to California to see her, or stay here until the Maud Allen sketch is produced?"

I swallowed hard to cover any break in my voice. "This is not for me to decide."

He knit his brow, then announced, "I will go."

"What about your rehearsals with Maud Allen and the performance at the Metropolitan? This is a great opportunity."

"You can rehearse Maud Allen while I am gone! Do it for me. Don't you see, I cannot stand it any longer. I have to appeal personally to Leslyn. I may even be able to return for the premiere of the play!"

Incomprehensibly tolerant and protective of him, I went to Maud Allen and explained that for a few days I would have to take Reginald's place at rehearsals. Since I had been helping him with rehearsals from the beginning, she did not seem to mind.

Claude Bragdon, the architect, came to see me the night Reginald left. He was also a mystic who wrote books about the higher consciousness and the unseen world. He lectured all over New York and was highly regarded for his wisdom. He told me I was perishing for want of a warm and vital love, although it really did not take a mystic to see that.

Three days later a telegram came from Reginald: "She does not love me. Am returning immediately."

Part of me admired Reginald's poetic extravagance of spending the money for a one-day trip to California. Yet it was a sophomoric gesture, the kind of thing young men imagined Shelley would have done. It certainly did not suit a person who read the Bhagavad-Gita and talked at great length about detachment. All I could do was laugh, almost wishing he were no longer in my life.

When Reginald returned Maud Allen invited me to Boston to see the preview production, but something made me hesitate. I told her I would let her know.

That afternoon I visited Benjamin de Casseres, the esteemed liberal journalist, and his wife. We had spent many evenings with them; Reginald was spellbound by Benjamin's erudition and language, and I was touched by how deeply he loved his wife. When I mentioned to them that Maud Allen had invited me as her guest to Boston, they raised their eyebrows and exchanged knowing smiles. "We never took you for a lesbian, Beatrice. Surely you know that Maud Allen is a notorious member of the Sapphic cult." So that was it! I declined her invitation.

To my surprise, Reginald did not seem desperately unhappy over his broken romance with Leslyn. He accepted defeat without a struggle, and for the rest of the winter we continued our close, but platonic, relationship.

In spring he returned to California and I pursued my interest in Theosophy. Robert Logan, a lawyer who had given up his profession and conventional society to dedicate himself to Theosophy, invited me to meet Dr. Besant at his home. Logan and his beautiful wife, Sara, were from old Philadelphia families. They lived in a large, historic house near Philadelphia which they had turned into a Theosophy center. Surrounded by several hundred acres, the house had priceless early-American heirlooms, silver by Paul Revere, pewter brought over by the Pilgrim fathers, and furniture by early-American craftsmen. On the morning I

left: Benjamin de Casseres, the esteemed liberal journalist, and his wife.

right: Dora Van Gelder, one of the finest clairvoyants in the world

was to meet Dr. Besant, a letter arrived from Reginald which left me shaken and emotionally fragile. He had met a young girl of eighteen. Though he mentioned it casually, I knew it carried unspoken implications.

Twenty of us were in the Logans' sitting room when Dr. Besant entered. She was dressed in white, said a few words to the group, then came over to speak to me. "I am glad Dora has a friend who understands her," she said.

She was referring to Dora Van Gelder, a fascinating young Dutch woman who was visiting me at that time. A tiny creature with a narrow, elfin face and slanting eyes, she was considered one of the finest clairvoyants in the world. In spite of her delicacy, she was forthright and outspoken. Married to Fritz Kunz, she lectured widely and became a president of the Theosophical Society. Many were in awe of her, and many were captivated by her charm. I treated her simply as a friend. If she wanted to discuss the best-looking waiter at the delicatessen, I was happy to oblige.

Dora told me that I had a great deal of green in my aura—the color of sympathy—but that it was too light, too diffused. She said that I was not organized enough and must become more hard-boiled. Then she added severely: "You also have a great deal of grey in your aura and you must throw it out." It was true; I was grieving over Reginald and grey is the color of grief.

I wondered if Dr. Besant, too, could see my grey aura. At the meeting that morning, she said many of us were ready to be drawn into closer studies and work, but others were not yet serene enough. "Some of you can take the summer for quiet thought and bring steadiness into your being. We will meet in the fall and see if you qualify."

I knew she meant me.

I wrote Reginald about the meeting and how I intended to work on controlling my emotions. After a flurry of letters, he wrote that I should come west without delay. I preferred not to see him, as I feared he might go off with yet another woman, but he scoffed at any suggestion and urged me to come.

Somehow I knew it would make for disaster, but I finally gave in to his request and got on the train. The moment we met our old intimacy was re-established. A few days later he introduced me to Frances, the eighteen-year-old girl he had mentioned in his letter. She was a tiny young thing, not pretty, but appealing. There was no reason to suspect he was in love with her. Still, I felt threatened.

It was like a well-known drama unfolding: I had read the book before and knew what the next page would bring. Reginald kept assuring me Frances meant nothing to him. At a picnic in Palm Springs with Frances and two other friends, the situation finally reached a climax.

I had a premonition and begged Reginald to go without me, but he insisted. When we arrived, we decided to go swimming. Frances appeared in a one-piece bathing suit, her slim, young figure like that of the wood nymphs who filled Reginald's Shelley-esque landscape. There was hardly a change of expression on Reginald's face, but he caught my eye, and in that instant both of us saw what the other felt.

It was like a well-known drama unfolding.

We sat on the rocks for luncheon. I was silent. An hour passed, and I announced that I was returning to Los Angeles. Reginald insisted on driving me part of the way back. On a hill some miles along we stopped the car and went to sit under a tree.

"It is true," he confessed, "I have fallen in love with her."

"Oh, Reginald," I moaned, "Why did you let me come west, when you know you were attracted to her?"

He protested with surprising intensity. "It is you whom I love. But her tiny figure, her innocent face, her strange mentality—they pull me to her."

I lifted my face to the pale sky; a soft breeze played around the trees, gently rippling the green leaves. "Reginald, there is one thing I want to ask of you," I began slowly, trying to keep my voice even. "You know that this summer I am going through a kind of probationary period, trying to keep calm. Last summer, you were infatuated with someone and it did not end well. I only ask that you do not plunge right away into the idea of marriage. That is all I ask—wait!"

"I have no intention of marrying," he answered soberly. "I would not think of such a thing for months."

He spent the next ten days constantly with me. The last night before I was to leave for Chicago for my interview with Dr. Besant's representative, I implored, "Whatever you decide, please do not write anything of a disturbing nature in the next few days. This may be a turning point for me. If I keep calm, I can be accepted for work. It is a trial period for me." Even as I spoke, I knew that my strength was to be tested.

I went to Chicago and was there when Dr. Besant arrived at the railroad station with Krishnamurti. Wearing Eastern garb, he walked through the throng of several hundred devotees who threw flowers at his feet. His face remained unsmiling, as he did not want followers. Later we met in Wheaton, Illinois, where ground was broken for the new Theosophical headquarters. One woman knelt before Krishnamurti, murmuring: "Jesus." He quickly made her arise; this was a worship he would not tolerate. With a wry chuckle I thought of Reginald's response to the woman in Hollywood.

On Saturday I told a friend, "I am expecting a letter today. It will be upsetting. Please understand if I am not myself."

The letter came. Reginald had decided to marry. I had been gone for five days.

On Tuesday I was to meet Dr. Besant's representative, Dr. George Arundale, later president of the Theosophical Society, who was to accept me for work providing I had grown in steadiness during the summer. I thought to myself, "This is it, Reginald will not wait, he will marry Tuesday, the day he knows is so important to me."

Tuesday the telegram came. He was marrying that afternoon at two-thirty. I was having my meeting with Arundale at two.

I went to bed that night filled with sorrow so overwhelming I thought I was disintegrating. But as the night wore on, I saw that there was a choice in my life.

Either I could cling forever to my despair, living in twilight, or I could leap into the very center of the flame, completely face my grief, and transcend it. I chose the fire.

Even stronger than my love for Reginald was my desire to make a tie with Dr. Besant. I could not go on being someone else's shadow. I got down on my knees and surrendered myself to an ecstasy of renunciation.

The next morning it was as if my aura, once violent and turbulent, had become peaceful. I was not the same person. Only memory without feeling was left of the past.

I Move to California

Puzzled as to how to pick up the pieces of my life, several things made me decide to move to California. Krishnamurti was speaking there, and the Arensbergs had settled permanently in Los Angeles. The land was beautiful and the city was wide open.

At first I stayed at a hotel downtown on Grand Street, but found myself more threatened by the neighborhood than I had ever been in New York or Paris. I spent late evenings with Lou and Walter, then took a half-hour streetcar ride back to my hotel. One night, walking along the deserted street, a man came up and walked beside me.

Lou, aghast, asked, "What on earth did you do?"

"I conversed with him as if it were perfectly natural to walk with him. I was frightened to death, but forced myself to appear calm." I paused to impress her with my wisdom. "I was careful, however, to walk on the outside of the sidewalk so I would not be near a dark alley. I put my purse in my outside hand so he could not easily grab it. When I approached the hotel I saw a watchman at the door and, before the man realized what was happening, I rushed in as if the devil were chasing me."

Lou and Walter sighed with relief, but pressed me to move nearer to them in Hollywood, which was safer.

I took a room at the Hotel Rector on Western Avenue. Every afternoon I took lonely walks into the hills, where there were virtually no houses. Vine Street was the end of the tramcar, and Cahuenga Boulevard was narrow and lined with palms.

It was three months since Reginald had married. When he heard I was in Hollywood he rushed over with his new wife to see me. He may have thought he was going to enjoy a harem, but the past was in the ashcan and, having no emotion left, I treated him like a good friend when he and Frances called. She told me Reginald had numerous photos of me in his apartment when he brought her there as his bride; I wondered how he had explained me to her. I never held Frances responsible for separating us and knew I could never do anything to hurt their relationship.

Reginald, Frances, and I had several friends in common, so we met often. I was perfectly comfortable in their presence and felt no emotional upheaval where Reginald was concerned. I was truly recovered!

Krishnamurti arrived in Ojai, California, in 1926. His first talks coincided with the opening of the camp there. Ojai is one of the most beautiful valleys of the world, five miles wide and surrounded by rolling hills and mountains. I am not surprised that it was once a favorite place of the Native Americans, who

Reginald, Frances, and I met often.

Though the paintings would have been extraordinary in a contemporary building, there was shock value in walking through the symmetrical bushes, ringing the bell of a traditional house, and finding oneself facing the chaos of explosive canvases.

held their peace meetings there. The Krishnamurti Camp was situated at one end of the valley, on a slightly sloping hill. Tents were put up to house visitors who came from all over to hear him. Many considered him to be the most profound speaker of the era.

I was happily looking forward to attending the camp opening when, several days before, Reginald phoned urgently. "You must get vaccinated for smallpox immediately. You and Frances were exposed."

Jenny, a woman with whom we had dined a week earlier, had come down with it. "It is terribly contagious," Reginald continued, "and you shook hands with her. Frances kissed her good night."

"But I don't want that horrid vaccine inside of me, especially when I am going to hear Krishnamurti."

He was annoyed. "Your choice then, but I have warned you."

I walked to the window, gazed out at the hills, and weighed Reginald's warning. I did not want to be vaccinated.

Then, one day before the camp opened, I came down with a cold. It was exactly two weeks since I had been exposed to smallpox—just the right time for symptoms to appear.

I took my concern to Mr. Louis Zalk, the camp manager. He was a man of extraordinary organizational abilities and integrity who had amassed a fortune, yet was also a poet. With Robert Logan, he later helped finance the Happy Valley School in Ojai.

Trusting his judgment, I explained my dilemma. "You have the responsibility to protect all these people, yet I ask you to give me this one day to see if I can get rid of this cold. If by evening it still persists, I will leave the camp." I wanted so to be present at the opening.

It was early morning. I fixed a jug of bicarbonate of soda, walked to a hill, lay down on the warm and good earth, and took a sip of soda every few minutes, lifting my thoughts fearlessly to the great sweep of sky. I did not want this cold and with every breath refused to accept it.

By early evening it was gone and I was completely well!

More than a thousand people attended the week-long event. Volunteers policed the walks and took care of the food, which was put on tables buffet-style and eaten outside under an arbor. The kitchen where the ladies worked was later remodeled and became the original Happy Valley School. Krishnamurti gave a talk every morning under the oaks, the large branches of which provided shade from the sun. Every night he lit a bonfire on the top of the hill and started the evening with a chant. Robert Logan would say a few remarks before the talks began. Krishnamurti asked me to put on folk dances, a task which I undertook with great joy.

This first camp was a wonderful experience for me. I listened very carefully to Krishnamurti, and though I failed to understand everything, the imagery of the words became a part of me and I felt expanded, transformed.

In addition to the spiritual experience of hearing Krishnamurti, I was also having some entertainment of a less enlightened sort at the camp. The husband of one of the women helping in the cafeteria told me he and his wife were separated and that he had fallen in love with me. Having been rejected by Reginald I responded to his attention, but I was not rolling in the bushes with him, as the jealous wife told everyone I was.

I took wicked delight in the dark glances and condemning eyes of those who were supposedly pursuing the path of non-judgment.

The camp was a unique experience. We were bewitched by the beauty of the enchanting valley and the presence of this great thinker from the East. Ojai had a unique aura of its own, for the mountains, with their gentle configuration, rewarded us with sunsets of remarkable blues and pinks, making our souls gasp at the splendor.

I longed to remain and live in Ojai, but I had no money. I was living on seventy-two dollars a month, and the ever present pain in my neck sapped my energy, leaving me too run down to pursue a job. Yet the days went by quickly. Alone, I entertained myself writing stories and drawing, or taking long walks in the uninhabited hills. I also spent a great deal of time visiting the Arensbergs.

When the Arensbergs moved to their new home on Hillside Avenue in Hollywood, there were hardly any other houses in the area. The closest neighbor was Dolores del Rio, the beautiful Mexican movie star. I saw the Arensbergs' new house the day after they bought it and could hardly hide my surprise that with their avant garde taste in art, they had chosen a conventional Georgian home with a stylized garden in the classical manner. They did commission the architect Richard Neutra to add a room to the sitting area, with large panels of glass opening to a small garden in the back, where reigned a stone Mayan princess. Walter was one of the first to collect Pre-Columbian art, encouraged by Stendhal, the art dealer, who with complicity and ingenuity sneaked treasures out of Mexico.

For the first time since they had left New York, the Arensbergs' collection of modern art had come out of storage and was again displayed. Though the Picassos, Picabias, and Duchamps would have been extraordinary in a contemporary building, there was even greater shock value in ringing the bell of a traditional house and finding oneself facing the chaos of such explosive canvases. A Brancusi graced the entrance; stepping under an old beam of wood, one entered the large square sitting room. Facing the door was the fireplace, hidden by another Brancusi—two marvelous torsos of lovers in stone, forever caught in embrace. Marcel's *Nude Descending a Staircase* had the place of honor on a wall shared with Picasso, while Rousseau, Miro, and Matisse hung with extravagance. No space was left uncovered. A yellow Miro took possession of one entire wall.

"I can't understand the Miro—it's just a scrawl," I told them honestly.

For the first time since they left New York, the Arensbergs' collection of paintings, sculpture, and drawings had come out of storage and was displayed again.

"Maybe with time I'll understand it . . ." Smiling at my ignorance, they changed the subject to my latest beau. They wanted to hear about every new man I met and insisted that I bring each one to meet them. I embellished my tales and enlarged the flirtations; I so appreciated the wealth of culture they brought into my life, I wanted to bring spice and entertainment into theirs. I think my daily absurdities were a relief to them after listening to some of their more highbrow visitors.

Though they were only about ten years older than I, they often treated me like a daughter. When I had colds they brought me food and took me to the doctor. They took a personal interest in how I dressed, which concerned them because I had so little money. The few dresses I had were hand-me-downs. One friend, who bought her clothes in Paris, gave me beautiful silken scarves after she wore them a few times. These would cover a tear or spot on my dress. In my poverty, what I longed for most was a piece of expensive scented soap instead of the Ivory I used!

I often wondered if they enjoyed hearing about my little romances because of the curious relationship they had. I could not fathom it. During the day Walter was furiously preoccupied with two secretaries deciphering cryptograms. During the night he and Lou shared a dark wooden bed together, circa Queen Victoria. And possibly their sexual relationship came from Victoria's period too, because somewhere there was a wall between them. In front of me they discussed Walter's amorous peccadilloes openly, referring to the fact that Walter had permission to visit these little chippies whom he paid. I listened, thunderstruck at these revelations, but never asked questions.

Then one night, to my shock and dismay, after driving me home Walter came at me with romantic intent. As I was getting out of his car he vigorously put his arms around me. "This is impossible," I objected, struggling to get out of his embrace. "We have been friends for years, let us not spoil our relationship." Holding me tighter he murmured, kissing my ear, "Lou allows me to have affairs, you know."

"But not with her best friend," I replied frigidly. "It's out of the question."

I squashed this little scene between us, and in the many years that followed neither of us ever referred to it again. But a few weeks after it took place the openness of their relationship was revealed to me when Lou said, "You are the only woman I know with whom another woman's husband is safe." Evidently he had told her everything. I treasured the sincerity and depth of her compliment.

The three of us loved fortune-tellers. Even though suspicious of them, we were hopeful. I went after card sharks, palmists, and clairvoyants, eager that their predictions would materialize some knight in white armor who would carry me off into the never-never-land of kisses. Lou sometimes went with me to the readings and afterward Walter would listen to our reports, trying to catch some convincing shred of sense in the nonsense we talked.

left: Walter was furiously preoccupied deciphering cryptograms.

right: Lou Arensberg

"In spite of the clap-trap of fortune-tellers, there really is a man chasing me," I told Walter and Lou one day. "He is married, and the other day he went into his 'my wife does not understand me' routine. I told him he should get a divorce if he is not happy, instead of continually deceiving his wife."

Lou sat forward, concentrating on my every word. I went on like a Salvation Army preacher.

"He kept telling me how much his wife loved him, therefore he felt he could not divorce her. We argued for an hour, then what do you think he told me?"

"What?" Lou could hardly contain herself.

My voice rose in a crescendo of laughter, "The jerk told me he wanted to stay with her because she set such a good table!"

We went into shrieks of laughter. "Into the kitchen stove with him!" I cried. "Into the kitchen stove with all men! They are only good to keep bugs off roses; the lady spider is the wise organism of the species, she eats her mate after the deed is done. Pimps, buffaloes, weasels, that is all men are!" Lou, still laughing, clapped her hands in agreement, and Walter, grinning rather feebly, reached for a pencil and escaped into his world of calculations.

Without the social life of New York Walter threw himself even farther into his search to prove that Bacon had written the works attributed to Shakespeare. Each new clue was greeted with the ecstasy of discovery, only to be quickly discarded as new clues emerged.

"I have almost solved it!" He repeated over and over, guilelessly every time, offering us a patient smile as we made fun of him.

Several years later, he found messages in the cryptograms from which he concluded that Shakespeare was buried in an incestuous position with his mother and that rare unpublished manuscripts were to be found in the grave. He set sail for England to see to the opening of Shakespeare's grave and to arrange for these great manuscripts to be given back to the world. The Archbishop of the Church of England, however, held another point of view. Walter returned to Hollywood earlier than expected. In many ways Walter, a poet from Harvard, was similar to Reginald, a dreamer from Cambridge.

I said nothing and contrived a Mona Lisa smile.

One morning, while reading on the sofa, I heard Reginald's footsteps on the front porch. He entered impressively, stood tall and ethereal at the foot of the couch, and started lamely: "Frances is right for me. I need youth." He waited for me to agree. I said nothing and contrived a Mona Lisa smile.

He repeated: "I need youth."

He waited for me to protest, but what could I say, I was still young myself. His eyes shifted, searching for certainty. "My marriage is a great success. Frances is giving her life to me."

That hurt. I, too, had given up my life for him—seven years.

"I need youth," he said for the last time. The more impassive was my face, the more I laughed inside. What can one do when one is up against the absurdity of life but laugh!

He sat down, told me he was not well, and asked my advice about a future operation. The hypochondriac he was later to become was beginning to peek out of its seed. I had no intention of giving advice. I wanted him to stand on his own two feet, but it became increasingly clear to everyone who knew him that he never would.

For years he had wanted to play the part of Christ in the Pilgrimage Play. Finally he was given the opportunity. A week before the play opened he came to call on me, adjusted his long frame into a narrow chair, coughed, and began in a low voice. "A clairvoyant told me that if I played the Christus, I will die at the crucifixion." His brows knit; he waited with an alarmed expression for the remark to sink in.

"Well?"

"What do you think I should do? Do you think I should go on with this part?"

"Why not? I can't think of a more wonderful way of dying." A terrible silence followed. I pursued: "We all have to die. For years you dreamed of playing the part. What could be more dramatic than dying on the cross?" Without consolation he went to other friends, but they too laughed at him. I waited to see how he would get out of it. To my surprise he went on with rehearsals and played the part for a week. The second week he collapsed with a cold. Though able to sustain long talks with me over the telephone, he did not have the strength to undertake the role, and with great condescension informed me his understudy would have to go on for him. The following night, however, he managed to make an appearance in the role, but the next evening, he again stayed at home to protect himself from the night air. The next day he phoned and in an incredulous voice said: "What do you think? They have fired me and my understudy is to act the Christus the rest of the season."

"Reggie, dear," I said, "how could you expect anything else?"

He was well enough the next day to be seen with a blonde in a vegetarian restaurant.

Galka

Now that the Arensbergs' paintings were again on exhibit in their home, friends began pouring in. Lou and Walter were generous about allowing visitors to see the collection and never refused a request from anyone. But for Lou it was a dreaded chore. Al-though she gave the impression of enjoying people, she was shy and had the kind of modest reserve that kept her from playing the piano in front of others, myself included, though she was an ac-complished musician.

When I met Galka Scheyer, she impressed me as the rudest person I had ever met.

One night Lou phoned me to come over immediately; a woman with a heavy German accent had arrived, and Lou wanted me to help her see the evening through. When I met Galka Scheyer I wanted to run, for she impressed me as the rudest person I had ever met. Short, with a large head full of dyed henna hair and Semitic features, the unconventional beauty of her face escaped me. Her voice was strident and her manner so intense it was abrasive. Yet she was so alive in a room, and scintillating, that no one else counted. I went home and scolded myself for so readily disliking this woman.

The second time we met I saw through her rudeness and perceived a person of enormous tolerance and dignity. She was like a gourd—rough on the outside, but full of rare delicacy within.

Galka Scheyer had brought from Germany the paintings of Paul Klee, Vas-ily Kandinsky, Alexej Jawlensky, and Lyonel Feininger. They were unknown at that time in America, but well known in Europe as "The Blue Four." Lou and Walter were immediately responsive to the paintings and helped her get an ex-hibition at a gallery on Vine Street.

For a time Scheyer was continually at the Arensbergs'. Along with Ruth Maitland, another collector, they consulted her continually. They appreciated her burning heart and valued the friendship of this extraordinary woman.

Walter and Scheyer would lose themselves in conversation about art for hours. Walter was starving for this kind of exchange. But eventually there was a disagreement over the sale of a painting and Lou, who found it hard to endure Galka's shrieking—or perhaps her artistic affinity with Walter—used it as an excuse to halt the meetings.

Scheyer bought a lot on top of the Outpost—a hill overlooking Hollywood—for two hundred dollars. It was reached only by a tortuously steep and winding road which Galka drove up at high speed. It terrified me.

Once there, if one could forget the ordeal of the trip, it was a paradise. She had asked Richard Neutra to design the house, which was actually one very large sitting room gallery used to display the Blue Four paintings. There was little furniture. To one side there was an anteroom to store paintings and to the other a small bedroom opening on to a garden. She had extraordinary taste. On the hills she discovered weeds and arranged them with decorative skill in empty pickle jars which sat on the floor. She opened the door of art to many, showing us a creative way of living. I visited there often and came to appreciate Klee, as well as American primitive and folk art.

Chez Scheyer

left: Sherrill Schell, the noted photographer from *Vogue*

right: Michael O'Shaunessey, the talented painter

Los Angeles was just stirring with its first interest in art. The movement was like the murmur of a giant in sleep. Museum directors, gallery owners, and the elite of the art world often met at the Arensbergs'. Rarely was Scheyer invited. Even though she knew far more than most of them, her manner put people off.

Not only would she take charge of the scene and dominate it, but her shrill voice was exhausting. Knowing her eagerness to be accepted in certain circles and her capacity for contributing ideas, I finally found the courage to tell her that she would be invited out more often if she would not shout so much.

She was outraged. "But I will shout," she shrieked, gesticulating wildly. "It is what I say that is important, not how I say it!"

That was the end of my efforts. She did not choose to change, or perhaps she could not.

The evenings at the Arensbergs' reminded me of the old gatherings in New York. Museum directors, collectors, designers of rare books like Merle—a book-seller from Texas who had his shop downtown on Hope Street—and my good friend, Helen Freeman, were often there.

Edward Weston came several times to show his new work in photography. He was a short man with a mild voice and personality. The memory of his wonderful prints, their tone and inventive compositions, came back to haunt me years later when I took up photography.

One evening, when the group was involved flaunting their erudition, I quietly remarked: "I read *The Ladies' Home Journal.* In it boy kisses girl and lives happily ever after. That is all I ask out of life."

Lou and Michael O'Shaunesscy, the young and talented painter—who had a crush on me—nodded their heads in delight. There was an excitement and enjoyment to the Arensbergs' Los Angeles evenings, but missing was the wild exuberance and youthful sense of revolt that had protested the evils of the jury system, or celebrated the originality of Brancusi, or pondered the mysteries of chess. It was not the same freedom of thought that helped us escape from the horrors of World War I; if those Los Angeles residents could not tolerate Galka Scheyer's outbursts, they would never have stood for the outlandish gestures of Mina Loy and Arthur Craven!

A Trip That Changes My Life

With my flirtatious nature, I missed masculine companionship and kept hoping a new love would break around the corner. Though still a fool about love, by this time I knew that becoming "one with another" is a momentary illusion. One is alone. A woman can get trapped into all kinds of relationships in her attempts to deny that realization. No longer was I willing to fall into a man's arms to escape the abyss, for having scaled the lower depths of that precipice, I had found my inner resilience even more powerful than the hug from a masculine arm. On those warm summer nights, as I sat on my patio, watching stars shoot across the sky, I wondered what it really meant to fall in love—was it just a biological trick to insure the growth of the human race or indeed what it seemed, a brush with the gods? I thought about love because I knew it would be some time before I would feel its tug again . . . but I fear I am just a marshmallow where men are concerned.

With my good friend Helen Freeman

No sooner had I resolved to live without love than I found myself engaged to Ralph, a slightly built, fair-haired young man who had been calling on me for some time. After months of talking about nothing but his girlfriend, he suddenly announced that he had fallen in love with me. Even though I did not feel any tug of love toward him, those three little words—"I love you"—succeeded in winning me over. However, I was soon leaving for Europe for three months with Helen Freeman. We had been invited by Krishnamurti to attend several weeks of pre-camp at Castle Eerde in Ommen, Holland, followed by another week of camp opened to the public. It was a privilege I would not pass up.

Ralph threw his arms around me. "Oh, you cannot leave me now!" he protested in a tortured voice.

"I promise I will come back," I assured him. "You need not worry, it is a promise."

I left for New York with the illusion that upon my return I would become a good wife and help raise avocados with my new husband. Both my mother and father came to the boat to see me off to Europe. Mother warned me against marriage with a man I did not love, and Father kept pressing dollar bills into my hand. This sweet gesture was the last thing he did for me. A few weeks later he died of pneumonia.

Helen's and my stay at the camp was not a great success. Dozens of people turned up at Castle Eerde uninvited and Krishnamurti refused to turn them away. Instead, a number of us were put up at a forlorn pension filled with old ladies. Two days after we arrived the rain started and we were chilled to the bone.

When I listened to Krishnamurti speak my attention was completely absorbed, but when I was alone the damp weather and guilt over having deserted Ralph dominated my thoughts.

Helen came and sat on my bed. Our conversations were often light and frivolous, but in the deeper realms of our beings the impact of Krishnamurti's thought continually broke through the banter. "What do you suppose Krishnamurti means when he says that the subconscious of man rises above the absolute to the heights of liberation?"

"I don't know," I said. I often struggled to understand him.

"He says that when man is untouched by the greed of the world, he finds himself released into unity, and then is ready to adapt himself to a spiritual concept."

I began watching the blue shadows on her neck. She continued, "Do you suppose the liberated man is conscious of the 'I Am,' whether the 'I Am' is apparent to himself or others?"

"He is superb and uncompromising," I said with true conviction. I wished my admiration could help me transcend my heaviness.

When the camp was over, Helen and I flew from Amsterdam to Paris. In 1930, flying was rather daring, especially in foul weather.

"I don't mind dying," Helen announced.

"I don't either," I politely agreed, "but I have my fiancé to consider."

As we rose high into the sky there were two rainbows over the earth. The airplane soared into the open blue and passed through puffed-up clouds that glistened as the sunlight touched them. I caught my breath with the magic of it all. There was such a feeling of pure life high in the clouds that both of us were in a trance. I thought of Krishnamurti. He and this radiance of the air were the same thing. Far down was the earth with its dirt, its sorrow, its passion. Here in the clouds was only joy and space.

I was brought down to earth upon our arrival in Paris.

Customs officials engulfed us. A coachman cursed because we had so much luggage. The hotels were crowded. In desperation, we took a dirty, grimy room swirling with red wallpaper and gold furniture. The sordidness was overbearing.

"If you were liberated and really understood what Krishnaji meant, you could stand any room," Helen admonished, plucking her eyebrows. "He says the liberated man is happy anywhere."

"Then I am not liberated," I cried. "If Krishnaji had to live in this room, he wouldn't be either!"

One hot morning, sitting crosslegged on her bed, wearing only a shirt and drawers, she was in the mood to refer to her occupation.

"Beatrice," she began in firm, staccato voice. "I am reading a letter from a man who is distraught over the loss of his son. I have written him that the son is fine, going on with his work and . . ." she paused, observing me wickedly, and continued. "Goodness, do you suppose the son can see me sitting here in my underwear!"

I moved to the window to pull back the curtain and announced, "A man across the street is peeking at us."

"Stop looking. He'll think you're encouraging him."

"I'm sure he thinks I'm studying to be a virgin."

That made her laugh. "Oh, you naughty girl, why are you so naughty?"

"I like to be," I answered, rolling my eyes around.

"Do you know why?" she said.

"No."

"Come here and sit down. I'm going to talk to you." I obeyed.

She smiled and shook her head slowly. "I'm going to disillusion you, and you're not going to like it. You're not as naughty as you think. You're conventional and somewhat of a prig, and just put on an act to cover it."

"That isn't true!" I cried, my cheeks becoming red.

"I know you. You try to shock others before they shock you."

"As soon as I'm dressed, I'm going out."

She went on relentlessly. "If you were really free inside, you wouldn't concern yourself with pretending to be the opposite of what you really are. You think that by facing the balance in one direction, you counteract the other."

"What are you going to do with me then! I don't want to be integrated. I don't want to be free of opposites. I want to be naughty and buy possessions for my house."

She came over and put her arms around me, and I felt her warmth. "You're an angel," I said in a low voice, as I rested against her softness.

"An angel who wears black tights," she answered sadly. "The least disturbance and the black shows."

—from *The Angel Who Wore Black Tights*

left: Elizabeth Reynolds Hapgood in Germany

right: Stanislawski demonstrates spontaneous makeup with clothespins and a handbag.

We had hardly fallen asleep when someone tapped quietly at our door. The reason was obvious to Helen, who grabbed my arm to keep me from getting up and answering. It was an assignation house. I put the pillow over my head and tried to go back to sleep.

The following afternoon Helen received news that added to our gloom. Unable to get a needed loan, she was forced to sail for America the next day.

The following morning was heavy with unreality. The day before we had planned to spend the day at St. Cloud. Now we were leaving Paris, each going a different way. "Goodbye," I said, my heart sinking. "Goodbye, little one," Helen replied wearily, and gave me a peck on each cheek.

Outside, the early morning light was cold and grey. The Paris streets were teeming with workers. A monstrous loneliness descended on me . . . then I was on the train, en route to Germany to visit Elizabeth and Norman Hapgood, who had rented a beautiful house in Freiberg.

Elizabeth was translating the books of Konstantin Stanislawski, the director of the Moscow Art Theatre, who was staying with them at their home in the Black Forest.

Stanislawski was a tall, thin man with white hair, an oval face which nurtured two wrinkles running down his cheeks. He was an impressive gentleman of the old school, with princely manners and eyes that danced with amusement when he talked. He entertained us by demonstrating the impromptu acting techniques he had done so much to develop. My Hollywood banter astonished him, but he was cosmopolitan enough to hide his surprise at my free use of words. He wanted me to visit friends of his in Italy, but I was not free to travel. I was engaged. I had made a promise.

Lying in bed that night, my emotions suddenly merged into focus and I realized I was not and never would be in love with Ralph. Was I out of my mind, thinking I could be happy with a man who wanted only to raise avocados, thought Cezanne was a brand of coffee, and had no interest in anything beyond the acres that enclosed him? His ardor and my love of romance had blinded me. Seeing this all so clearly, I wanted to write him that we could not marry. But how could I write such a letter when I'd promised that I would return?

Filled with regret, I gave up Italy, hugged the Hapsgoods, had my hand kissed by Stanislavski, and returned to California.

Ralph met my train at Los Angeles. When I saw his ineffectual face and blond moustache, I had no second thoughts about my decision.

That evening I slowly broke the news.

"I have come back . . . as I promised . . ." I faltered, hating to hurt him; then forcing myself to continue, "I have come back to tell you that I cannot marry you. I am not in love with you."

The pupils of his eyes became small, he swallowed, and a strange smile came to his face. I waited. Then, he shrugged his shoulders, tilted his head, and declared arrogantly, "That's all right, I can take care of myself." His jaw tightened and a dark expression came over his face. "I'll just go get myself another girl."

I was staggered by his quick recovery. I had ruined my trip dwelling on him, and given up seeing Europe with creative people to honor a commitment that was founded on a faulty premise! It was a painful lesson: I should have been honest in the beginning instead of the end. It seemed as if my trip to Europe had been a complete failure. In fact, it was to profoundly change the course of my life—but in a way I never could have anticipated.

My first experiments in pottery date back to 1933, when I enrolled in a ceramics class offered by the Hollywood High School Adult Education Department.

In Holland, I had been spellbound by the antique stores that lined the squares, and had spent hours picking out copper and silver and tiles. In Haarlem, I bought six plates with a beautiful lustre glaze. Back in Los Angeles, I decided I wanted a teapot to go with them. Frustrated at being unable to find one anywhere, a young actor friend of mine, Morgan Farley, suggested I take a ceramics class at Hollywood High School and make one myself.

The next day I enrolled, expecting to make a teapot in twenty-four hours. I made two plates—both horrors—then modeled two figures which, for some inexplicable reason, someone bought. Thereupon, with my arrested financial brain, I reasoned that if I continued selling my pieces I might supplement my miserable seventy-three-dollars per month income. I became infatuated with clay and glazes, and spent the next three weeks in the library reading back issues of the *Ceramic Society Bulletin*, hoping some of the information would sink into my unconscious. It certainly did, but my primary concern at that time was economic, not artistic. The Depression was on.

I remember leaning out the window of my Gower Street bungalow and seeing a well-dressed young man approach. On the spur of the moment I asked him if he would like a sandwich, and to my surprise he answered that he would. Handing it to him through the window, I could hardly believe that a man of such distinctive appearance was hungry. At least I had my seventy-three dollars a month. Rent took a third of that, and the rest went quickly for food and doctor bills.

I continued to need medical attention for my neck. I went from one doctor to another, from the finest orthopedic specialists to the most notorious quacks. There was a physician from Vienna, to whom Aldous Huxley and other well-known people went for treatment, who gave gold injections as a cure for every ailment. A friend arranged for me to see him without charge, so I got shots of gold in my hip for the pain in my neck!

For months I went to another handsome osteopath named "Red." From my meager income I paid him large sums of money, but when I accidentally pushed a sewing needle into my knee he coldly suggested I go to the general hospital where they would remove it for free.

I drove miles to the hospital, holding my knee straight so the needle would not move. It was grim registering as a charity patient and sitting for hours in a dark hall, amidst the moans of other patients with far worse afflictions than mine.

Finally I was ushered into a small booth with canvas walls. A young intern gave me a local anesthetic, had me hold a cardboard in front of my eyes, and began probing the knee. Soon he announced he had taken the needle out and left. The nurse came back and whispered that it was still in my knee. It is to this day!

In an effort to earn money, I applied for a job giving French lessons to a movie star. She lived in the Beverly Hills Hotel in a barren room full of dust and flowers. During the interview the muscles in my neck became so spastic that I could not hold my head up straight. Despite my perfect French, I was not given the position.

It was at this time that Helen Freeman made a remark that changed my thinking. I longed to have a bottle of inexpensive toilet water, but refused to buy it.

I had such difficulty learning how to drive. But once I did, I drove seventy miles an hour all over. When I got a new car, I went into the flat desert and drove eighty miles an hour! I was stopped by a very handsome policeman. I batted my eyes and said, "You know, this is a new car. I'm used to my old car and one doesn't realize how much faster these new cars are." I did not get a ticket.

"You are attached to poverty," she scolded me. "You cling to *not* having. It is just as negative as being obsessed with wealth."

She was right. It was a matter of attitude, and mine presumed deprivation. I determined to take the first step toward changing my disastrous financial state. I let go of poverty—at least, within. Without, however, I was still dependent on the generosity of Elizabeth Hapgood and my father's secretary, who sent large checks at Christmas and on my birthday

I often considered the women in my life—my mother, Helen, and Elizabeth—and realized how profoundly they influenced my behavior and attitudes. I saw that the conflict with my mother was like a fire in which my mettle had been tested. I rejoiced in my loving friendships with Helen and Elizabeth, both women of enormous talent, spirit, and generosity. It was at this time I met a fourth woman with whom I would enjoy a deep, life-long bond of affection and respect.

Rosalind

Rosalind Rajagopal was a strikingly beautiful American girl with blond hair, enormous blue eyes, Grecian features, and a wide, generous mouth. She had travelled with Dr. Besant and studied under Charles Leadbeater, then an Anglican bishop, in Australia. In the twenties, Rosalind had been engaged to Nytyananda, Krishnamurti's brother; after his death, the newspapers tried to link her romantically with Krishnamurti, but her marriage to D. Rajagopal put an end to that. Rajagopal was a brilliant young Indian, educated at

Rosalind Rajagopal

Cambridge, and at one time considered a candidate for prime minister of India, but he chose to dedicate his life to Krishnamurti and his activities. Rosalind kept house for both men, and for many years Krishnamurti, Rajagopal, and Rosalind lived as one family.

Rosalind's sister, Erma, was responsible for Krishnamurti coming to Ojai. Erma was tutoring in the Ojai Valley and told Dr. Besant that the climate would be good for Nytyananda, who was suffering from tuberculosis. A friend donated a ranch, Arya Vihara, for the brothers to use, and Dr. Besant bought land at the other end of Ojai for the camps. Robert Logan bought a large house at the back of the property.

Krishnamurti had a little house behind the main one. Few were allowed to enter it, but once I saw it while it was being cleaned. The rooms were barren of all except the simplest pieces of furniture and scrupulously clean. Rajagopal's modern house, designed by Jon D. Davidson—in which the archives were kept—was close by.

Though I admired Rosalind from a distance, I was too shy to approach her, and we met only a few times when Dorothy McBrayer brought the Rajagopals to dinner in my little garage apartment on Gower Street in Los Angeles. One night I found her gazing at Rajagopal with the most beautiful smile of love and tenderness. Like a curtain lifting, I saw into the soul of another human being and from that time I became her loving and adoring friend. We began to see each other frequently and, at one time, decided to go into the dressmaking business together. The birth of her child, however, changed our plans.

Rosalind's daughter, Radha, was an enchanting and wise child. I remember standing by her cradle while her mother, father, and Krishnamurti were admiring her. The child seemed wiser than all three of them put together. She had a unique quality and Rosalind brought her up wisely, taking her to Europe and on whatever travels she undertook. Krishnamurti loved the little girl, helping with her upbringing almost as if he were a second father. Unable to pronounce "Beatrice," she called me "Beato." I started using the name to sign my work and close friends call me "Beato" to this day.

For many years, Krishnamurti, Rajagopal, and Rosalind lived together, Rosalind keeping house for both men.

I enjoyed the lucidity of Rajagopal's mind, his meticulous pursuit of perfection. He had a little book in which were names of everything published about Krishnamurti and the places where he had lectured. We were much impressed with the efficient way he kept Krishnamurti's files. At all times he knew where lectures were held anywhere in the world, books published, and expenses incurred.

Steve

Arriving at friends for dinner one evening, I found a tall, gangling man waiting at the door. I was disappointed; Steve Hoag was pure Yankee, not my type. But when I sat down next to him at dinner, I noticed his fine eyes deep set under bushy brows, his honest gaze, and wondered what it would be like to go to bed with him. His remarks were intelligent, expressed with wry humor. He had an original way of keeping the conversation going and his deep voice held much kindness. Trained as an engineer, he was now a real estate appraiser and considered one of the best by his colleagues. He was the kind of escort mothers liked for their daughters. Proper and well mannered, he was like a fixture at local debutante balls.

Steve Hoag

I was the first artist he had ever met, and just as I was attracted by his incredible conformity, he was attracted by my lack of it. But on our third meeting, as I crossed the street against the light, he swore at me in such bad language I vowed never to see him again. An hour later he phoned, and in the gentlest voice begged: "Do not pay attention to the way I swear. It is a habit I have indulged because there is no wife near to correct me. It has become a part of me. All my friends are used to it and laugh it off." Marshmallow that I am, I immediately forgave him; a mistake, if ever I made one.

Steve might not have lasted long in my life, but he had a head for finances, and that was a gift I could hardly overlook. One day I was struggling to balance a checkbook. "Here, let me do that," he proposed. "I am good at figures."

"I do not like people to know how I spend money," I replied, weighing the temptation of help against the invasion of privacy.

"I will never pay attention to what you spend," he impatiently reassured me. "I will balance your checkbook and never look at what you spend." From that time on I let him balance my checkbook and I never wrote a check that he did not complain about my extravagance.

With some trepidation, I took Steve to meet the Arensbergs. Steve sank his lanky frame into an overstuffed chair, stretched out his long legs in front of him, dropped his head on his chest, and thus remained in a state of hibernation, without saying a word, for the rest of the evening.

Driving back I scolded him: "What is the matter with you? Usually you are talkative and outgoing with people. Tonight you were not only silent, but impolite."

With a growl he spat out: "How do you expect me to talk in front of those god damn pictures? I've never seen anything like them in my life. The Arensbergs must be crazy."

I told him that if he wanted to be a part of my life he would have to learn about my world. He agreed to read art books, and the next time we returned to the Arensbergs' I watched him from the corner of my eye as he explained the quality of a painting to another guest. He took others on a tour of the collection, expounding on the genius of Picasso and Brancusi.

In spite of Steve's willingness, he did not fit into the social evenings there. His brusque honesty was a liability. Once, at a party where an opera singer performed, Steve announced loudly, "Noise, noise, it's just noise."

There was laughter, but not from me. Eventually, I exiled myself from the Arensbergs' wonderful evenings and saw them only when they came to see me every several days. Yet I kept my association with Steve. After the tortuous love affairs I had endured, Steve's security was a respite. We met on rock, not sand. We certainly felt a kind of affection for each other, but not love. Whatever it was, it was also platonic. He never made a pass, and when I put an affectionate arm around him, he tossed it off with annoyance. He was not homosexual, nor sexual at all. He suffered with prostate and hernia troubles which, as a Christian Scientist, he ignored—until he discovered that Veteran's compensation would pay for a hernia operation! However, my exuberance exhausted him and he dismissed all my ideas, big or small.

"Why don't you buy a piece of property?" I urged him. "Land is cheap in the San Fernando Valley. Take out a loan and build a duplex and I will be your tenant."

After months of resistance, Steve finally bought a small lot on Sarah Street, in what is now North Hollywood. The lot had seventy-five feet of frontage, tall eucalyptus trees, and a small ditch at one side. We discussed the ditch, which was a shallow six-foot wash. We were assured it was safe from flooding. Months passed before there was enough money to begin construction on a house, but at least he had property.

I met Steve's friends, all stuffy, except for Jack and Frances Case, whom I liked the moment we met. They were up-to-date, liberal people in their forties. Jack had been an Olympic hurdler, travelled with the team to Russia, and met Frances in Paris. After living together for two years they decided to marry "for

top: Jack Case

below: Frances Case

right: They often invited friends to join them on the weekends in Del Mar.

the convenience," the trap of all who love. They were cosmopolitan enough to enjoy Steve's unusual character and appreciate his integrity, even though he was an incurable conservative. Steve's political views were in such opposition to mine that I automatically voted against whatever he advised, without even studying the issue.

Jack, now a successful advertising man, and Frances leased twenty acres down in Del Mar, California, near the beach. They often invited friends to join them on the weekends to partake in life *au naturel*. The beach was deserted and no one paid any attention, except the conductors on the Southern Pacific Railroad.

I, however, the liberal one, having seen nude models since I was sixteen years old studying art at the Julian Academy in Paris, could not get myself into the ocean without a bathing suit. Even Steve did not hesitate to plunge in naked. I was still attached to the inhibitions of my youth and following the stern moral admonitions of my mother.

My mother was much in my life at this time. She was dying of cancer and had come to San Francisco to be with her sisters. She faced her death heroically and rarely referred to her illness. I went to San Francisco every few weeks and we began meeting on new ground, one without barriers. She finally realized she had misjudged me. We even began sharing a sense of humor. The morning of her death, I found her on a narrow couch, white as a sheet and motionless. Only her eyes moved from side to side, more brilliant than I had ever seen them. I approached her bed, holding out my hand, and said with a grin, "I have a little present for you."

She opened the tiny package in which I had put a piece of chewing gum. She burst into laughter. Mother was the last person who ever would have chewed gum. The rest of the family was horrified and thought my gesture obscene, but my mother smiled and said, "Beatrice is the only one who understands." I did. She and I knew that one can do nothing in the face of the ultimate but laugh.

I was with her later that night.

She murmured, "Are you going to leave your name in the social register?"

"Mother, I am not social. It holds no meaning for me."

After a few minutes her eyes sought mine. "You need never worry about money. In a month you will have fifty thousand dollars and next summer, when the city condemns our houses to build the new bridge, you will have thousands more and be well off." I sat in silence, watching her, beautiful as marble, at peace. Once more her eyes flickered and partly rising, she tried to smile. "Oh, am I still here?" she said. Her smile faded and she sank back into a coma. The last thing she said, to herself, was: "Oh, it is so beautiful, so beautiful."

I was completely prepared for my mother's death, yet it was the most awful shock. I wished I had told her that I would leave my name in the social register— such a simple lie to ease the passage to the other side— where I hoped no social distinctions existed.

I soon discovered that financial comfort was not to be a part of my future. Knowing nothing of business, mother had put heavy mortgages on the properties and all was lost. I salvaged only two railroad bonds worth one thousand dollars, and therefore was unable to buy the lot from Steve, as I had originally intended. Months dragged on while he tried to arrange a loan so we could pay the contractor to build.

One evening he came by to tell me that the contractor wanted an answer within forty-eight hours. Steve had only one hundred dollars to his name, but a deal in escrow which would bring in several hundred more once the account closed. I urged him to make the commitment. It was our only chance of having a house, and the only way I would have a place to work on my pottery and thus earn an income. But he felt it was too great a risk. If the deal in escrow fell through he would lose the lot altogether. I accepted his decision.

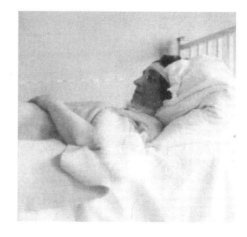

I was completely prepared for my mother's death—and it was still an awful shock.

The shop at Crossroads of the World

The next morning Steve came by to see me on his way to work. He had decided to take the gamble. He wanted me to have a chance at my pottery. The decision revealed the true generosity of his character and fortunately his deal did come through.

While the house was being built, Crossroads of the World, a development of small artisan shops on Sunset Boulevard in Hollywood, rented me one of the stores for a discounted rent of twenty-five dollars a month. Moroni Olson, an actor who had performed with Reginald, loaned me two-hundred and fifty dollars to see me through the first six months, and Elizabeth Hapgood sent me one hundred dollars for a kiln. In those days there were no kilns for sale; they had to be custom made. My first kiln did not work and the crook who built it disappeared with the check. This did not stop Elizabeth from backing me in a second kiln, for she was determined to get me on my feet.

In those days no one was making pottery and decent ceramic materials were simply not available. In spite of the crudeness of my pieces and bad glazes, my figures sold. One, representing the Duke and Duchess of Windsor, attracted many to my shop window, and each month I was able to pay back part of my debt to Moroni.

When the house was finished, I found myself with a large sitting room, bedroom, kitchen, and dinette. Steve had a small bedroom, bath, and private entrance. It was palatial in contrast to the way we had been living.

We agreed to live separate lives, each with our own friends and activities. Our relationship remained platonic, which now suited me. I was too absorbed in pottery to complain. At my little shop in Hollywood I was experimenting with decent glazes and also beginning to make a profit beyond the loan.

Then I suddenly developed a severe pain in my side which slowed me down. Elizabeth, an angel on the warpath to see me succeed, insisted I build a workshop in back of the new house and sent more money. Steve and Jack Case designed and helped build the room, and I gave up on the shop and moved into my own place.

It was February 1938. Toward the end of the month rain began falling like a grey curtain. It stormed for two weeks and the ground was saturated. I walked out under the eucalyptus trees and stood on the wash, watching the water slowly running down. To my horror, I saw the earth falling into the water and phoned the highway department for sandbags.

In the late afternoon it started to pour again. I worried and slept in my clothes while Steve laughed at my apprehension. By dawn the wash had become a torrent. I began putting furniture on top of tables, in case the water reached the floor of the house.

Steve grumbled at my absurd concern and neighbors shrugged. The waters grew fiercer, the wash larger. By five o'clock, neighbors conceded that it might be wise to move the furniture and cars to a higher street. In the darkness came a shrieking sound. One of the eucalyptus trees went down like a match, born away by the torrent. Soon another popping noise and a second tree went down, and a third and fourth. The raging, snarling waters were now at the doorstep of the workshop. A shattering noise of wind arose and in one gulp the workroom disappeared. I watched without feeling—in a disaster feelings disappear.

Neighbors on high ground invited us to their home for the night, though I sensed it was with gritted teeth, for everyone assumed Steve and I were living "in sin."

Eleven of us were marooned, cut off from the rest of the Valley; bridges were down and no rescue teams could reach us. The night was dark without electricity and the storm shook the house as we stretched out on the floor, trying to sleep. At one o'clock in the morning I heard an angry clattering noise and saw a flash of lightning. In that very moment the river took our house in a single gulp.

The waters were still rising, and I knew if the rains continued the house we were in would also go down in the savage current.

The next day the rain stopped and the sun came out shining. It was the third of March, my birthday. The trees, workshop, house, and even the land had been swept away and destroyed by the deluge. Only a row of flowers was left, defying disaster.

The Arensbergs volunteered to put us up for the first few days. I arrived mud spattered, unwashed, and uncombed, the sound of roaring water still beating in my ears. At dinner Walter remarked, "We have been all day with decorators, for we are doing over one of the rooms. You know the color of the wallpaper is very important."

How could wallpaper matter when my home, my workshop, my hopes, and my future were gone? Suddenly I saw how relative everything is. Wallpaper is important to one who already has security. I had none. I had fifty dollars in the bank. Yet never had I felt so free, my only estate being my spirit and the air I breathed. I

Steve and I in front of our second home, 1938.

had faced death; now I faced life and with every breath I felt fulfilled.

Gela Archipenko—the wife of the famous sculptor, Alexander Archipenko, and a fine artist in her own right—generously invited us to share her apartment. She was a tall woman with classical features, her dark hair parted in the middle and caught in a knot at the back. We stayed with her for some time, until Steve found a small house for us. Gone, I thought, were my ideas of ever making pottery again.

Hearing there was a disaster fund for flood victims, I encouraged Steve to investigate. He had registered for assistance, but when the Red Cross invited him to come to their office, he hesitated. I decided to go myself. The Red Cross officer, Miss Selby, listened attentively as I answered her routine questions. Walking with me to the door she remarked, "I will see what can be done. But do not raise your hopes. Maybe we can get fifteen dollars to replace your glazes. I doubt that I can manage much." Steve's skepticism was right. Fifteen dollars!

Three weeks later Miss Selby phoned. "Miss Wood, I am glad to tell you that the disaster fund of the Red Cross is giving Steven Hoag nine hundred dollars to buy a new lot, five hundred dollars for you to start a new workshop, one hundred twenty-five dollars for a new kiln, plus a hundred dollars for materials."

Weakly I gasped, "I don't believe it, you must be kidding."

"No, it's true, we are giving more for the lot than Mr. Hoag paid because prices have gone up and we are allowing more for your workshop because this time you will not have friends to build it and you will have to employ labor."

Thus, the Red Cross enabled me to pick up the broken pieces of my life. It was a gift that had no measure. In spite of this generous aid it was six months before we were able to buy a new lot and break ground. Steve found one with apricot trees—on higher ground.

Ironically, the disaster afforded us a better home and studio than we had before, but in other realms the mortgage on my life was immense. Steve convinced me that the Red Cross would not knowingly provide a grant to rebuild a house to two people who were not legally married. I, of course, had no compunction about taking the government's money. If doing so without being married constituted fraud, so be it. But Steve had more integrity than I did. He did not want to lie to the Red Cross, and he liked the idea of marriage. I brought considerable warmth and companionship to his life at a time when he was feeling increasingly isolated due to a loss of hearing.

We argued for days, and in the end Steve's view prevailed. I was not secure enough to give up the only chance I had for rebuilding my studio. Once again I agreed to get married, with the provision that we could later have it annulled.

A moth-eaten justice of the peace married us in Las Vegas with two seedy underworld types as witnesses. I had such a fierce headache after the ceremony that I wished I were dead. We agreed that we would tell no one about the marriage, for we planned to continue living independently. I particularly wanted to keep the marriage a secret from my aunt in San Francisco. I was due to receive an inheritance when she died and was certain she would never allow it if she knew I had tied myself to a man without an estate of his own.

Beatrice Wood in Central Park, 1927

Pottery Becomes Serious Business

Once again I was married, and in name only. But I had my pottery workshop and was able to continue my experiments. I would not say I had great gifts as a potter, but I organized myself to become one. I was obsessed with learning, and would station myself at the wheel and work with the kiln for hours.

Glen Lukens, the noted craftsman, was teaching at the University of Southern California, and I happily enrolled in one of his courses. Though I was not his most talented student, I was the hardest working. In the end, it is only hard work that counts.

I was born on March 3, under the sign of Pisces . . .

My studies continued with Gertrud and Otto Natzler, the Austrian potters who emigrated to California in 1940. Gertrud had a genius for throwing wonderful shapes on the wheel, sensitive and reaching for the sky, and Otto was no less accomplished in technical matters. My apprenticeship with them was one of the happiest times of my life, and their teaching was an important influence during this period. I was so eager to learn from them that I sold some of my books to pay for the lessons.

The Natzlers raised the standards of pottery in California and helped to elevate pottery from the status of a craft to that of an art. Their ceramics have been exhibited all over the world. Gertrud taught me how to throw clay on the wheel, and Otto taught me how to keep accurate records of the precise mixtures I used in every glaze. No one taught me as much until I met Otto and Vivika Heino, with whom I later studied.

The Second World War was on, merchandise was scarce, and before I was truly professional, I began getting wholesale orders from such stores and galleries as Bullocks Wilshire, Neiman-Marcus, American House, Gump's, and V. C. Morris. Mrs. Aileen Vanderbilt Webb, an important figure in the craft revival in America, had a shop on Madison Avenue in New York managed by Frances Wright, the daughter of Frank Lloyd Wright. For several years they gave me an open order every other month which I filled with shipments of ceramic figures, vases, and decorative plates.

My workshop in the early days

In 1943, Frances Case approached me to help her assemble a group of craftsmen to attract business to the Town and Country Market, across from the Farmer's Market in Los Angeles. This was one of the first merchandising strategies devised to promote crafts in Southern California. Frances, a young woman of vivid imagination, told prominent citizens that the craft group was just a stepping stone for a museum of modern art and, thus, was able to collect important names for the board of directors. She failed to mention that the Museum of Modern Art in New York was started by twenty millionaires each donating a large sum, while this board of directors was assured no money would be asked or needed.

Her vision was exciting, but misleading. Dorothy Liebes, the great weaving designer, was asked to be a director. She phoned long distance to warn me that the business setup was not sound.

I immediately told Frances, but she thought my alarm was exaggerated. So a beautiful house of cards was built. One important person after another was told that certain names were on the board when they had not yet accepted and, thus, an impressive group was assembled: President of Lockheed Robert Gross; Sumner Spaulding, eminent architect; Mrs. Rudolph Liebig and Ruth Maitland, both collectors; and, of course, Walter Arensberg. The museum idea developed while the craft group became incidental.

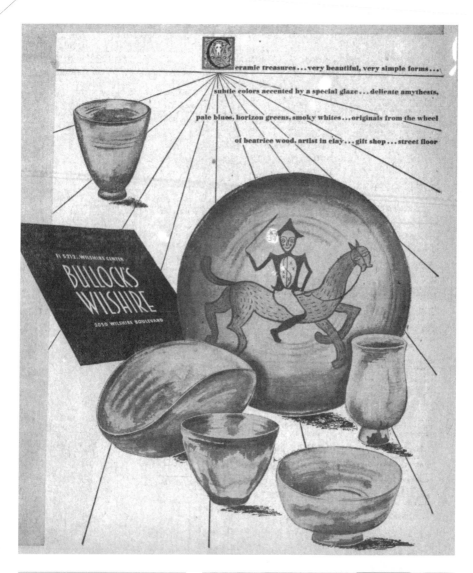

"Cat in Night" decorative plate, awarded $100 by Richard B. Gump at the 11th National Ceramic Exhibition for "the best ceramic design suitable for mass production."

We recruited fifty of the finest craftsmen in Los Angeles to join Arts in Action, and began preparing objects for the opening. While the Town and Country Market was ready to turn over endless space to the group, it did not choose to put up the money needed to build shelves for displaying wares—a sum of five hundred dollars was needed.

Every few days impatient craftsmen were assured the money would be forthcoming as soon as the board had its first meeting. When it finally met not a word was said about money, as I suspected would be the case.

Ruth Maitland was a dear friend, and I decided to explain the situation to her without delay. I drove to her home in Bel Air, where hung Picassos, Miros, and early Italian primitives, and told her the craftsmen needed five hundred dollars for shelves.

An unhappy expression drifted over her face. She said weakly: "We were assured that no money was needed."

I hated talking about business, especially to a friend, but forced myself to continue: "I was sure not a word had been said, and I felt that you should know what was needed before becoming further involved, although sales will quickly reimburse this small sum."

Haltingly, she explained that she and Walter Arensberg had only joined after assurance no financial demands would be put upon them. Soon they both resigned, furious at the misrepresentation. Despite their resignations, Frances decided to go ahead with the opening and somewhere found the money for the shelves.

The project attracted considerable publicity, and would certainly have been a sound financial venture if there had been either a dedicated board or good management behind it. It stayed open several months, with crowds coming and sales increasing, but the board lost interest as soon as the idea of a museum of modern art faded. Despite its failure, it had firmly established that a market for fine crafts did exist in Southern California, a market that Hatfield, the dealer in the Ambassador Hotel, and others were soon to develop.

My approach to art was on the snob side, for I had seen much of the finest. I had to drop this limited point of view when I became judge at the Ventura Fair. Seven Chinese figures from the same mold with different colors were presented to me for judging. With the full dignity of a museum connoisseur, I exclaimed: "These are from the same mold, I can't judge such things." An official approached and whispered: "That is not the way we evaluate entries. You must see that these figures are the first gesture toward esthetics from the rancher's wife and at that level you must evaluate them."

Once again on my own, I started a small factory and ended up tangling with Uncle Sam. I designed a few clowns and circus figures for mass production, received orders from department stores, invested in a kiln, and encouraged two craftsmen to make figures from the molds.

It took just a few weeks to realize that my little factory would not run smoothly unless I were there myself, which defeated the purpose, so I gave it up. Two months later, the Internal Revenue Service summoned me to their offices, where a stern-faced man snapped questions at me: "Where is your social security number? Where is your Board of Equalization permit?"

I had no idea what he was talking about. I was fined two hundred fifty dollars, wiping out my profits. Crushed, I wanted to fly away to Singapore.

Later a businessman bought my clown designs, took over the equipment, and was to give me a percentage on each figure sold, but his lawyer was smarter than mine. Thousands of clowns were sold without the assured percentage to me. One little word—"net" or "gross," cunningly placed—made all the difference.

Twice more big business sought me out, and again with sorry results. Finally I vowed to take commercial matters into my own hands. Delivering my pottery to a store, I received the surprise of my life. The salesgirl asked, "Where is your invoice?" her eyebrows arching as she unpacked my treasures.

"Invoice, what is an invoice?"

An agent had always done this for me.

"A list of the merchandise you are delivering."

Drawing myself up in utter disbelief, I announced, "I am an artist, not a typist. I do not make invoices."

She picked up a pad and smiled: "Sit down and I will explain the facts of life. How do you expect us to pay you, if you do not give us the list of what you have made?"

I saw that I would have to get off my high horse and meet the world on its own terms. I drew up my five feet, three inches into seven feet, four inches and changed from a dreamy girl into a business-minded person, meticulous and accurate. Accepting discipline, I entered the world I had run away from home to find out about. I saw that no one is in isolation, and that there must be a technique of communication where commitments are involved. For if one is not exact reality is unforgiving, and one of the reasons our world is a mess is that man will not keep his word. From that time on I have made invoices so exact that museums have remarked that no artist ever delivered clearer ones. Such compliments please me more than praise about a bowl.

In addition to perfecting my skills as a potter and invoice maker, I studied painting with Galka Scheyer. Though she was especially interested in teaching children, she started a class for adults which she gave at my home. It had been Steve's bright idea that she should hold her class at my place and pay rent. Because I would not think of charging her he complained constantly.

The purpose of the class was to free individuals for creative expression. Everyone was allowed to paint the way they wanted—except me. Because Scheyer and I were such good friends, she was not detached where I was concerned. She, who stressed freedom for everyone, would not let me paint the way I wanted and insisted that I change my style. Since I could not talk her down—no one could—I took vengeance by drawing vulgar ladies of the night, a phase that annoyed her and gave Rosalind—who also took the class—moments of sorrow. Rosalind revealed the talent to be a first-rate painter, had she wanted. But then, it is my opinion that Rosalind could be first-rate in anything she undertook.

Scheyer loved to teach, and though I teased her with rebellion, I learned a great deal from my association with her. She made me see that the accident often provides desired effects in art and pointed out that the Japanese treasured the flaws in a glaze.

Steve did not get along with Scheyer. Both were masters of bad language and neither wanted to yield to the other in championship. Much as I loved

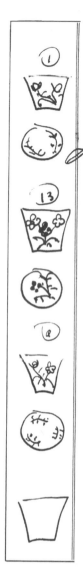

... I was just like a bride who does not know how to boil eggs. She becomes a good cook by experimentation; that's how I became a potter. I'm not a chemist, but then, neither were the early Chinese.

Scheyer, I had to admit she had a talent for antagonizing others. Steve was ornery enough without having her shriek at the same tempo. One evening she came to dinner and was helping me rearrange the furniture in the living room. We were enjoying ourselves when Steve strode in, his eyes blazing like an eagle after prey. "I said dinner is waiting," he raged.

"Let it wait," replied Scheyer in a voice topping his.

"God damn it, you bitch, I said dinner was ready!" shouted Steve, ready to assassinate her.

"God damn you, stop talking to me like this!" countered Scheyer.

They approached each other face to face, Steve towering over Scheyer, while I fled the battlefield, gliding to the kitchen. When both were so hoarse they could no longer yell they meekly came to the table, sat down, and began amiably conversing as if they had just been introduced at a dinner party. Scheyer never bore a grudge, nor did Steve. They simply felt entitled to be rude whenever they wanted, which was most of the time. In fact, they genuinely admired one another.

One day Scheyer telephoned Steve in a panic. She had been in an automobile accident and wanted him to come and help her. Knowing his ability, she wanted no one else to advise her. Deeply concerned for her well-being, Steve left without hesitation.

When he asked how the accident happened she rolled her eyes, shrugged, and blurted out: "I was driving on Wilshire Boulevard and a man from a side street came through without paying attention to the stop sign and rammed me."

"Didn't you glance at the street and see him approach?"

"Certainly not! The sign was there. It was his business to watch for me, not mine to watch for him!" she answered indignantly.

Scheyer had no sympathy for ill health. She was convinced my neck affliction was psychosomatic and twice made me go to European specialists, a handwriting expert, and a Rorschach test specialist.

She had even less tolerance for her own problems. I was with her at the hospital when the doctor told her she had cancer. She accepted the news calmly and then, with charming willfulness, turned her back on death. She did not want cancer and refused to accept it. She informed everyone she had no such thing. We saw her fade week by week. Friends, Ruth Maitland, Marjory Eaton, and Helen Freeman went to see her continually, keeping up the bluff with her. Doctor Knauer, with whom she was feuding, met me on the street and said: "Tell Scheyer to try a Viennese treatment. Otherwise, there is no hope."

When I gave Scheyer the message, with what strength she had left she shouted: "But what does he mean suggesting such a thing!"

Doctor Knauer finally decided to call on her; after all, they were old friends. He told her to stop her nonsense and accept death because the end was near. Like an obedient child she dutifully complied.

I like to brag that the Pasadena Museum (now the Norton Simon Museum of Art) only received her wondrous collection of paintings because of me.

She often spoke of her desire to leave her Klees, Kandinskys, and other paintings to the museum. She and the Arensbergs wanted both collections to remain in the West, but they could not come to an agreement about how it could be done. Since she was continually making changes in her will, I finally warned: "If you really want Pasadena to have the paintings, you must sign the will without delay." I did not want her to know how little time she had left, so I went on lamely: "Life is uncertain for all of us, any of us can go any moment. Now behave yourself and get it out of the way. Sign your will not tomorrow, but today."

The next morning the will was signed.

The morning she died, she was alone except for a new nurse who was on the case. Scheyer was conscious to the last. Her brain was active until she could no longer breathe. Peacefully, she murmured to the nurse: "Now I die and I am all alone."

The nurse replied: "You are not alone. God is with you." Scheyer's last words were a message to Walter Arensberg, with whom she had shared such a deep and loving friendship in art. She crossed her arms over her chest and managed to whisper: "Tell Walter there is no afterlife. I do not see it." Her eyes shut and she was gone.

The Long Road to Ojai

At Arya Vihara, Krishnamurti milked the cow and in every way was a working member of the household.

Friends in Hollywood were excited whenever I went to Arya Vihara, and asked me to listen carefully to everything Krishnamurti said so that I could report back to them. At first I went to Ojai expecting to hear talk of "higher" matters, and was surprised to hear conversations that revolved around Rosalind's vegetable garden and the cow. Krishnamurti milked the cow, and went around the place in blue jeans and a huge Mexican hat. He helped with the dishes, and in every way was a working member of the household, rather than a privileged person. We admired his simplicity and many of us were surprised when, in later years, he adopted a luxurious style of life.

Many felt a close tie with him, and some women even became infatuated with him. I never did. It was his teachings that moved me. But one day I had an urge to draw attention to myself. I walked up to talk to him as he stood alone, and started a conversation about my beautiful roses. He turned and stared at me as if he had never seen me before. I stopped mid-sentence, and in that moment of terrible silence died of embarrassment. A friend explained that Krishnamurti had no ego, and therefore could not respond when someone tried to attract attention to their own.

These weekends bore a certain disappointment. I longed to discuss such things as the third aspect of the Logos, or the coming of the Sixth Root Race, but conversations usually dealt with human affairs, and the activities were unpretentious and ordinary. In fact, everyone loved games, especially "Monopoly." One night Rosalind, who was a real shark at real estate, got everybody's holdings and even bankrupted Krishnamurti. I sat there paralyzed with boredom when Krishnamurti, catching my distant gaze, suddenly threw up his hands and said: "Beatrice has no idea what this is about and never will. Don't bother with her anymore." I was enormously relieved to withdraw myself from the encounter, which went on for three more hours!

Because of the war Steve had left real estate and gone into airplane designing, where he did excellent and ingenuous work. Everything was going well until he broke his hip. As a Christian Scientist, he went to a practitioner who wrote him a letter which he kept re-reading. "Know that you are now waiting in God—and that He does not take away all the senses. Look high and far, your Father loves you very much and is constantly with you."

The pain continued for three weeks.

Finally he went to a doctor and had x-rays, which showed that the hip was broken. Surgery followed, but since he had neglected it for so long the tissue was damaged. From that time on he was bent and in chronic pain. He had to give up his job, and I suggested that he become my manager and take care of materials, mix clay, and do odd jobs in the workshop. I should have had my head examined! He did not like pottery and, being in constant pain, was annoyed by my energy and creative vitality. So much of my strength went into appeasing him that it was difficult for me to meet my many orders.

I went and spoke to Krishnamurti about my problems with Steve. Krishnamurti never told a person what to do, but he had an extraordinary ability to help individuals discover the basis of their problems.

I made notes following our conversation.

Beato: I do not get along with Steve, I know it is my own impatience. But to know this is not enough. It is too strenuous to maintain. You as a Brahman are conditioned not to like dirt. I am conditioned not to like irritability.

Krishnamurti: When you deal with people, you must become very still. Be firm with them and do not allow them to misbehave, or you spoil them.

Beato: Relationships are difficult for me, especially with Steve. There is the conflict of my work with its pressing demands, and the interruptions of his slow tempo, unwillingness to get work done, and his lack of interest. I am silent when I work, and I have my work organized.

Krishnamurti: Where then is your conflict? Think!

Beato: It is between Steve and my work. They go in two different directions.

Krishnamurti: Then your problem is occupation versus relationship. What is the real problem underneath?

Beato: To make the two meet.

Krishnamurti: But they cannot. They go in two different directions. Your work then is an escape. You are seeking satisfaction in it. You want result, fame, and recognition. In your relationship with Steve you demand comfort, return. Now what are you going to do about it?

Beato: Just as awareness of virtue means awareness of viciousness, I see that I must live in a state free of demands. But I get tired, exhausted, and there is nothing left—then Steve talks to me in his loud deaf voice which sounds like a fog horn and I cannot stand it.

Krishnamurti: But can't you go away for a rest?

"Ah yes," I replied to this very practical suggestion. But it would begin all over again as soon as I returned. What I really wanted was to be free of my

left: Several friends told me I should try to be more conventional in my attire. I was accused of always being in costume. I went out and bought a tailored suit. Four months had passed, when one day I realized that I had withdrawn into a shell. Puzzled, it suddenly occurred to me that I was subdued because of the suit. I felt uncomfortable in it, totally not myself. From that time on I made up my mind that I would dress the way I wished.

right: My dachshund Dali

marriage to Steve. Though he was a good soul, and a sentimental man who openly wept when our pet cat died, he had become completely dependent. Cranky, deaf, and suffering with his hip, his only hobby was nagging me.

I longed to move to Ojai, which infuriated him. He made me promise never to buy land without consulting him, for he was knowledgeable concerning real estate and was terrified that I would make a bad deal.

In 1944, after a weekend in Ojai, Willie Weidman, who was also in real estate, drove me to the bus and casually remarked, "Only one lot is left here on McAndrew Road."

"Which lot is left?" I asked, hardly able to contain myself.

He slowed the car. "That one."

It was "my lot," the one I had always wanted. "How much are they asking for it?"

He told me.

"I'll buy it," I replied, without knowing where I was going to find the money. I had one hundred dollars in the bank and two railroad bonds from my mother's estate. In that instant I reasoned that if I threw them into the deal, I would have enough to put down a deposit. Then, if necessary, I could go out and wait on tables or scrub floors.

I cried excitedly, "I'll give you a check right now as a deposit. In two days I will let you know how much more I can put toward the sale." I wrote him a check for twenty-five dollars!

Remembering my promise not to buy property without consulting Steve, I knew there would be trouble when I faced him. "Steve, I have bad news for you. I have bought a lot in Ojai, one square acre—a lot I have loved and wanted for years."

He started to protest. I went on, "I did not mean to buy property behind your back. The opportunity arose and I seized it. Next week we will drive to Ojai and I will show it to you."

I was cagey enough, however, not to drive there alone with Steve. I took Helen Freeman with us. She and I chatted gaily in the front of the car, while Steve sulked in the back.

When he saw the lot, undeveloped land covered with rock and brush, he gloomily remarked, "All it has is a view."

"Exactly!" I laughed.

"It might have a subterranean river for all you know," he went on morosely, enjoying his gloom.

"Wonderful luck if it had," I rejoined, stepping over a rock and getting a cactus thorn in my hand. "The lot is in my name. You are not involved financially, so you need not worry if I have made a mistake."

Rosalind invited us to tea, and was so kind and attentive to Steve that on the return trip he actually smiled twice.

At last I had my lot, though there could be no thought of building until the war was over. While I did not experience this war as deeply and directly as I had World War I, my life was certainly touched by it, in both difficult and amusing ways.

I took in a young Mexican boy to help keep the workroom in order. He did not speak English and said he had come to this country to learn the language. I tried to teach him simple words, but he was not an ardent student. Yet I noticed he wrote many letters home. He loved my little dachshund and enjoyed taking her for walks when he mailed his letters.

After a few weeks he suddenly left one night, mumbling something about a man he had to meet without delay. A month later, two men from the FBI arrived at my door. Standing there in my kimono, I gushed with excitement. Very casually they asked me numerous, irrelevant questions, then said: "Does your mother live in Europe?"

"Don't bring my mother into this," I said, both outraged and amused. "She has been dead several years." They then wanted to know if I knew anyone by the name of Dali. "Indeed I do," I laughed, and called out to my darling dachshund, Dali, who doddled into the room. They patted her head and soon left, telling me nothing of their reason for coming. A few days later they called on Steve and revealed to him that my nice Mexican boy had been a go-between for exchanges of letters from foreign countries. Evidently my house, with friends and visitors from all over the world often calling, was a perfect setup for spy activities. Out of curiosity, I phoned the butcher and asked him if my Mexican boy spoke English when he came to pick up meat.

"Better than I do," he answered. "I always wondered why you kept phoning me as if he did not understand . . ."

I also had interesting experiences with my Japanese employees, whom the government had recently released from concentration camps in the United States. Although my neighbors objected to having Japanese people near while we were still at war, I was happy to employ them.

The first was George. Having worked for years as a bellhop in hotels, being stuck in an isolated place such as mine, with a woman continuously covered in clay, was a real letdown in excitement for him. After one week, he announced he was leaving. However, that evening friends drove up in a luxurious limousine and I greeted them wearing a silk dress. The next morning George announced he would stay. He stayed several months, taking care of my workshop and garden. He especially loved the big cars of friends who came to visit, and thus reassured his status.

"I never leave you. You like sister to me. My friends make more money than me. I no care," he told me. He did not care until he met Isha, a Japanese woman who, as he put it, "changed his shoes."

I understood. He left to marry her.

Then came Henry, also released from a concentration camp. He was a man of dignity who had been a merchant, never a servant. Having come to America as a young adult, he still held old world sympathy for his country and was convinced Japan would never surrender. His pride never bothered me. He was gracious and honorable. Short and wiry, his face was full of lines, as if he were constantly sucking in his cheeks. He treated me like a child, telling me what to eat and when to work. He sternly disapproved of my notion to move to Ojai, which pleased Steve no end. A few months later, I was working on the wheel when over the radio came the horrendous news of the first atomic bomb being dropped. I knew it would end the war. I went to the kitchen and gently told Henry.

"Japan never give up!" he insisted and walked away. I ached for him.

The day Japan surrendered Henry sat at the kitchen table, overcome with grief. I stood by him, wanting him to know that by my presence he had a friend, and in the silence between us neither was an enemy.

One day Reginald's wife, Frances, came to call on me. She knew I liked her and held no bad feelings about the past. She sat down slowly, smoothing her dress.

"I am going to divorce Reginald," she announced. "I love him, I will never

love another. But he will not work, and
I do not want to spend the rest of my
life legally forced to support him."

The words floated away in thin air.
For a long time there was not a sound
between us. She wanted my advice,
but I had none to give. It was between
her and Reginald.

They divorced; later she married
a musician, moved to New York,
and had a son.

If Reginald had any idea of
returning to me, he knew he did
not have a chance with Steve
camped on the doorstep. But the

Rupert Pole and Anais Nin.

moment he was divorced, he began coming to Ojai on the weekends and writing
me letters about his son, Rupert, and of Rupert's association with Anais Nin.
Anais, a beautiful, tiny woman with an oval face, delicate features, strange mysterious eyes, and a feminine mystique was a close friend of Rupert's. She was
generous and encouraging to young writers and, though we did not meet often
during these years, our friendship was close and understanding.

Anais Nin's diaries are highly esteemed as great literary creations, yet
Reginald was always condescending about her writing, undoubtedly jealous of
her accomplishments and popularity. He wrote:

Dearest Bea: I'm still rather down and very easily tired. The difficulty is that I am
so often helpless by myself. Rupert and Anais will be back on May 4th from their
trip to the West Indies. Anais is charming and interesting, but not interested in
anything but Rupert and her work. I still have the old car, but it is very insecure.
I don't see any way of seeing you this weekend. I feel so utterly disconcerted
(physically) and lost. I do want to see you and have a good talk, so much, so much.
I shall come to see you, if necessary in a bus. My dearest love to you. I do want
so much to come, and shall soon.

His letters did not move me.

Ever since buying the lot in Ojai, Steve had constantly quarreled about making the move. "I am an old man; you are dislodging me from my home." Fed up,
I told him that if he did not want to move I would give him my interest in our
house in Los Angeles and move to Ojai without him. Jeanne d'Arc, leading the
French, could not have been more determined than I was.

Fearing that I might leave him, he finally surrendered. We still had to wait another year before all the financial arrangements could be made, which meant securing a loan and mortgaging our other house. With the move imminent, I decided the time had finally come to annul the marriage to Steve. It would be an enormous relief, but it was not an easy subject to bring up. I hesitated to hurt him, but there was no use delaying the inevitable forever.

Lloyd and Helen Wright (Reginald's first wife) and their son Eric.

Steve knew I had gone through the marriage ceremony only on the condition that we could have it annulled. After some protesting he agreed to keep his word. We found a lawyer who assured us there would be no difficulty, since the marriage had never been consummated; I wondered how the law ever verified such assertions. All would have been easily settled, except for a legal fee of five hundred dollars, which could not be spared. We did not even have that kind of money to put toward the escrow account. We remained married.

When Helen and Lloyd Wright heard I was moving to Ojai, Lloyd said he would sketch out a floor plan for my new place. He was a very accomplished architect, and it has always been my belief that had he not lived in the shadow of his father, he would have been more recognized for his talents.

I objected. "I cannot afford an architect," I told him. "There is not one cent of extra money!"

I tried to discourage him, but Lloyd insisted that he would make only a sketch. So the three of us drove to Ojai and had a picnic on the lot. Lloyd fell in love with the site to such an extent that instead of just preparing a sketch, he presented me with pages and pages of beautifully finished blueprints.

The house he designed was charming. It had fieldstone walls, three baths and, to be economical, a workroom with walls composed of cheap materials like those used in chicken houses.

Steve hit the ceiling. "We can never afford to carry out his plan. The cost of fieldstone is prohibitive. Besides, Lloyd is crazy to suggest chicken wire for the workroom—anyone can poke a hole through it." Since Lloyd did not want to supervise construction, Steve and I agreed that we would quietly change the plans to suit our budget. Steve took the blueprints to Ojai and conferred with the carpenter, doing the best he could to lower the cost. Exasperating weeks passed. Each time Steve made a trip he cut out some of the design to get the estimate down. The fieldstone went first, followed by the third bathroom.

So much time was spent haggling that interest rates went up and we found ourselves short $2,500. With heavy heart, I gave up the plan.

***

In 1943, I went to New York to attend an opening at the American House, where some of my ceramic work was being exhibited. Wide-eyed, I stared at the city skyline, shuddering at the high buildings, the streets that had become stone canyons into which the sun never reached. It was not the same place where I had spent those daring, romantic days.

I was in the balcony of the America House when I saw Marcel Duchamp enter the gallery. I rushed down the stairs to greet him and we embraced as old friends. We had not seen each other since 1936, when he visited Los Angeles and stayed with the Arensbergs.

He made the rounds of the exhibit, complimented me on some of the conventional bowls, and took me to meet Rose Fried, who had an ultra-modern avant garde gallery. She too was responsive to what I had done, and remarked that my pottery was unlike any that she had seen. Marcel grinned happily at her reaction.

His loft on 14th Street had the same disorder as his apartment on 67th Street—the bed unmade and bits of chocolate lying around on the window sills. He showed me a chess set he designed. "You could make money if you marketed this," I exclaimed. "It is a wonderful idea." He answered with a slight smile, "What would I do with money?" The shadows from the street played on his face and he added, "I have enough for my needs. I can give all the French lessons I want. If I had more money I would have to spend time taking care of it and that is not the way I want to live."

In the few days I spent in New York I saw Marcel several times. He took me to luncheon at the Museum of Modern Art with his friend, Mary Reynolds, whom I found exquisitely feminine and well bred, quite unlike the women he had once preferred.

I also went to visit dear Elizabeth Hapgood, and once again her generosity and support enabled my dreams to come true. At dinner I happened to tell her how my plans to move to Ojai had been spoiled by the increased interest rates. Next morning at breakfast she entered with a check for $2,500. "You wire that contractor to start as quickly as he can."

Stunned, I replied, "But I can't take such a loan from you. My father taught me never to borrow from a friend." With blazing eyes she retorted, "If I cannot trust you, there is no one in the world I can trust."

Deeply moved, I accepted the check. Of all the people I knew, many sympathetic to the Ojai dream, none offered help as much as Elizabeth.

Back in California, I remarked to a friend that we were ready to build, but that we had made changes in Lloyd's design to meet construction costs.

"Did you tell Lloyd that you were changing his plans?" my friend asked.

The question haunted me all night. The next morning I went to see Lloyd and told him we had made the changes. He was angry. With my voice breaking I tried to explain, but I could understand that from his point of view we had destroyed his work of art. He offered to supervise the construction, but the carpenter was a quarrelsome old Scotsman who did not even know how to read blueprints. Lloyd dismissed my explanation. "Would you rather move to an ugly house than wait three months for a good one? During that time I will find an able contractor." But it was imperative that I get to Ojai; for weeks I'd let my wholesale orders slide and my finances were terribly low. I did not have enough money to wait. Lloyd swept out of the room. In tears I went to Lou and Walter and wept on their shoulders. Lloyd's beautiful plans were put away and I made a simple design in their place.

Several days later ground was broken. Every three days either Steve or I drove to Ojai to oversee the construction. One day I went up and saw, to my horror, that the exhibition room was laid out much smaller than planned. Upon returning home I told Steve and he explained, in a loud voice, "I changed your dimensions because you could not afford such a large room."

Color drained from my face. I held my hands tightly together to keep control. Steve knew that the show room was the heart of the house. I would have given up anything to keep its size. My business could not expand without that space. At my wit's end, I told Steve he would have to take a room in the village in Ojai. With or without an annulment, the separation had to be made. I would have a life of my own.

Wanting to leave my North Hollywood house spotless for the new owners, I asked an old Mormon woman to show me how to clean. "It is wonderful to put dishes in suds and have them come out sparkling," she said. "It is wonderful to have bathrooms clean, a bowl glistening, and the bathtub without a ring." She brought grace to housekeeping, and her loving point of view changed my outlook on chores. I spent three happy weeks scrubbing every room in the house. I washed walls, ceilings, windows, waxed floors, and made the closets spotless by putting fresh paper on the shelves. Today friends laugh when I say I would be happy just to be a housewife, but it is true—if I had a husband to keep my feet warm at night.

With a car laden with furniture and two howling cats, I started for Ojai—and a new life.

BEATRICE WOOD

When Marcel heard I was having an exhibition of pottery at the American Gallery in Los Angeles, he made a revolving fish design to go on the cover of my announcement as a surprise for me, and wrote the director:

"March 12, 1955 I hope to see Beatrice here very soon—and won't speak to her about the cover of her catalogue. But here it is: The "Roto-Relief" of a fish turning in a bowl (on a long-playing Victrola)—you also get a sensation of depth when the whole design revolves at 33 turns per minute. Please reproduce the design in black and white or in colour if you think it fit for the catalogue.

Good luck!
Sincerely,
Marcel Duchamp"

PART THREE

Beatrice Wood, *Not for the Innocent*, 1989. Pencil, pastel,
and watercolor, 17" h x 11" w

Reaching Rainbow's End

Ojai was the pot of gold at the end of a long, obstacle-strewn rainbow. From the moment I arrived on March 3, 1948, time ceased. The fact that the house was grim, with unpainted brick walls, did not matter, nor that the rocky acre did not have one blade of grass. The only living thing was an "old man cactus" I brought in a pot. Before unpacking I planted it, and in the next twenty years it grew six feet. I rushed to a nursery and bought two eucalyptus trees, painted the gray exterior of the house pink and blue, and then did what Frank Lloyd Wright asserted was a crime—I planted rose bushes and vines all over the place to hide its barren and bad architecture.

Ojai gothic

I arrived in Ojai with only enough money to live on for three weeks. With a second mortgage due from the old house I could not yet afford to complete the new one. For six months I ate in the workroom, for there was no kitchen, and slept in the exhibition room because there was no bedroom. I did not care. At last I was in Ojai, surrounded by luscious hills.

The very first day, someone came and bought pottery, and several other sales followed during the month. Steve came often to have dinner and seemed to be getting used to the separation. But after three months he pleaded with me to let him take the guest room. "It has sunlight and there is none where I am staying. I promise I will never bother you. I will never say a word to you again."

Steve was old and deaf and I was a marshmallow. I could not enjoy my view and sunlight when he was unhappy in such a dark place. I weakened, consoling myself that he would only live another year or two. He lived twelve.

Steve moved in and my new life of peace and solitude ended.

With the money from the sale of the North Hollywood house I planned to add a kitchen and dining room. I did not like eating in the workroom full of jars and lead glazes.

"But certainly you don't need a dining room, too," Steve argued.

"But I certainly do. Visitors will come from Los Angeles and I do not plan to feed them in the kitchen." We fought for hours. His mind always went toward security. So did mine, but having none, I gambled when opportunities came. Actually, his chronic opposition was the best thing that happened to me, for it forced me to become strong and decisive. Stirring the hot plate on which I was making soup, and brushing aside powdered glaze from a plate, I exclaimed: "I have no intention of spending the rest of my life dining in a room full of chemicals."

When I remarked to the foreman that I wanted a double sink in the kitchen, Steve exploded: "You crazy bitch, god damn you. What do you want a double sink for?" The workman, stunned, dropped his tools and came to my defense. Steve meant no harm. He swore in all kinds of hues and dissonances, anywhere, anytime, and neither my anger nor embarrassment had ever been able to change him.

One day an elegant lady came to buy pottery. She had entertained the Prince of Wales in her home and let me know it. While considering a golden bowl, Steve shouted to himself in the workroom nearby: "You god damn son of a bitch, you bastard, where did you put that tool?"

The lady stood without movement, mouth open, her bosom expanding with shock. "Who is that dreadful person?" she demanded, her virtue having been violated. In a weak voice I told her it was a workman.

Reginald occasionally spent time with us. He was a hypochondriac of the first order.

My peace was further disrupted by Reginald. He occasionally spent time with us, sleeping on the couch in the sitting room, and though I firmly told him the room had to be presentable for visitors in the morning, he would sleep until noon. In addition he did not make his bed. On top of this, he was a hypochondriac of the first order. We once counted nineteen bottles of medicine by his bed. He insisted that night air was bad for him and nailed blankets to the windows to keep out air and light. In this closed atmosphere he burned foul-smelling medicine. As a guest Reginald was a disaster. A letter from a good friend of Reginald's, Ed Weinig, indicated that his other hosts had the same reaction:

Dear Beatrice:

I saw Reginald Pole for about thirty minutes last Monday afternoon and wish to report to you.

He smoked some kind of cigarette for emphysema and the odor in the room was almost unbearable for me. The windows were all tightly closed with bedspreads hanging over them. Food of days ago was scattered about the room and on the bed. Reginald was in bed, lower part pajamas, upper part shirt and tie awry.

He told me all the "hard luck" stories, including:

1. His doctor was out of town.
2. Rupert was vacationing somewhere in the South Seas.
3. He cannot write, except does manage to sign his name.
4. Cannot walk more than a block or two.
5. Was confined to a sanitarium for two years as a result of taking too many barbiturates . . . was released by a court, I believe he said.

Then he turned to some kind of life after death, and strongly recommended that I read "The Betty Book" by Stewart Edward White. Reginald expected to meet us all after his and our death.

Perhaps all that I have written above should not be told . . .

Later Reginald wrote me:

In April I worked all the time coaching Charlie Chaplin's son, Syd, in Shakespeare. (Charlie asked me to.) If I am well enough I hope to do a production with him in the early Fall. I do want to see you very, very much, if you had an extra room with a panel ray heater like Steve has, I could come and stay.

Will Krishnamurti be at Wrightwood this summer? I have important issues to thrash out with him before I lecture again.

Again he wrote, suggesting I ask Steve to move out and let him take the guest room. Much as his loneliness saddened me, there was no place in my life for this man who still behaved like a young, bedridden child.

The Happy Valley School

The Happy Valley School was started a year before I moved to Ojai. It was one of the projects of the Happy Valley Foundation, an educational institution founded in 1927, by Dr. Besant, Krishnamurti, and Aldous Huxley. Dr. Guido Ferrando and Rosalind Rajagopal mapped the direction the school would take and the curriculum and polices that it would adopt.

It was ahead of its time, giving no grades and wanting no competitive spirit, co-educational and international, with the aim of developing well-balanced and creative individuals.

When the school opened at Arya Vihara on McAndrew Road in the east end of Ojai, it had nine pupils, including the Rajagopals' daughter Radha. As enrollment grew, the school moved to what had been the kitchen when Krishnamurti held the first camp.

The morning assembly started with silence, followed by peaceful music and the reading of a philosophic passage. Some felt the school should be labeled a Krishnamurti school, but he did not want it to be known as his, nor have his writings read. He suggested instead that only books of deceased authors be chosen for the morning reading.

Rosalind with Radha and Robert Logan

It was not easy for Rosalind, but she functioned with quick vision, going through one problem after the other. Krishnamurti came down with a kidney infection and she nursed him, for he would have no one else near. In the midst of caring for him, as well as the students, she broke her ankle and sometimes had to crawl on the floor to reach his side.

She volunteered her energies with single-minded devotion to the school. Rajagopal, her husband, also worked without salary, dedicating his time to arranging lectures all over the world for Krishnamurti and to organizing the publication of his books. Krishnamurti, talking to the staff, often recognized Rosalind and Rajagopal, and said the school would not exist were it not for them.

Robert Logan, a close friend of Krishnamurti, was a great contributor to the Happy Valley School. With Louis Zalk, he had started an endowment fund. As president of the Anti-Vivesection Society, an organization devoted to the protection of animals for use in experimentation, Louis had profound respect for all life. One day, as I swatted at an annoying fly, he admonished me not to kill it. "All animals love their lives, just the way you do yours."

It forever changed my attitude. I have, since then, enjoyed the task of catching moths or bees trapped in the house and letting them free outdoors.

Robert thought doctors were in league with black magicians and made Mabel, his loyal and protective secretary of many years, promise never to bring one into the house. Instead he went to a chiropractor who was violent, and Robert,

I taught pottery at the Happy Valley School for a number of years.

who was in his late seventies, came home unconscious after a treatment. Rosalind, over Mabel's protestations, insisted that a doctor be brought in to see him.

When our beloved Doctor Rupp appeared, Mabel met him at the door and informed him that Robert was already under a doctor's care. Dr. Rupp merrily nodded, ignored Mabel's remarks, and went to work bringing Robert back to consciousness. Dr. Rupp was a humanitarian with a sense of humor and honesty. When he did not know the answer to a question, he readily admitted it. For many years he was on the board of the Happy Valley Foundation, and his judgment was highly valued.

Another influence on the school was Aldous Huxley. He and his wife Maria, who was close to Rosalind, often came to Ojai. Aldous had long talks with Krishnamurti about education, and for fifteen years served on the board of the Happy Valley Foundation.

For many of us in Ojai, life centered around the Happy Valley School. I taught pottery there for a few years and discovered that everyone has innate talent, if released. Having no formal training as a teacher, I focused on imagination rather than technique. I told my students:

Educate your eye, go to wonderful museums, absorb the magnificent culture that has been built up through the ages. Spend time in libraries, look at art books. Culture is the meeting of minds; when a spark is born, one man adds a pearl to the chain of another. Do not imitate, but listen to the small voice which is your own and true.

Though I no longer teach, I would give the same advice today!

Another very special place in Ojai was the now famous Ranch House Restaurant. It began as a simple family project. Its owners, Alan and Helen Hooker, lived in the oldest house in Meiners Oaks, on a small hill above the Happy Valley School. Hospitable by nature, they continually invited friends to dinner. Alan loved to cook and was a wonderful host. The evenings proved so delightful that friends kept coming back—so often they insisted on paying something. We ate at one long table which Helen decorated beautifully with branches, weeds, and wildflowers. Eventually Alan decided to open a restaurant and Rajagopal sold him an acre near the Happy Valley School, thinking it would be a nice vegetarian restaurant where students and their parents could dine.

With the vegetarian menu Alan had trouble making money, so he expanded the menu to include meat and gourmet dishes, and fine wine. Soon the restaurant developed a swank reputation that attracted people from Los Angeles. In her column, Sheila Graham reported Paul Newman as saying it, "served the best food in the world."

Shopkeeping

When I moved to Ojai, I intended to find myself a business manager. I thought they grew on trees, just as I had once assumed that everyone had ten thousand dollars a year. Though Steve took care of the books and swept the workroom, his deafness and stooped posture made him ill-suited to deal with the people who came to the studio. I had no choice but to interrupt my work and greet the public.

I did not enjoy selling my work. One man complained, "Tell me something about the bowl. Sell it to me."

Feebly I replied, "I don't know what to tell you," and let the man walk out. I could not pressure people to buy; it just was not in my nature to market myself. Sometimes I succeeded despite my nature!

Standing in front of the sign advertising my first Ojai studio, 1956. Today my work is still sold at prices both "Reasonable and Unreasonable."

My first big sale was to a short, thin, overdressed man who came with his genial wife. While she chose pottery he stood by, his face pinched and formal. I tried to talk to him, but he kept backing farther into the wall. His wife bought several pieces, amounting to the unheard sum of four-hundred-fifty dollars. I acted as if it were peanuts.

After they left, I rushed into Steve's room and, in excitement, cried, "What do you think of this check, can it be good? It has a funny name that I cannot pronounce . . ."

Steve put on his glasses and grumbled, "What's the matter with you? Christ! It is from Zellerbach. You bet it's good!"

"Zellerbach. Who is Zellerbach?"

"He is president of the biggest paper company in the country." And here I had feared they might be con artists!

On another occasion a couple walked in and the wife pointed to a bowl. "How much is that?"

"Seventy-five dollars." Just as I was about to tell her there were less expensive things in the next room, her husband asked about a pair of kissing fish.

I did not want to sell them, so I priced them at an exorbitant three-hundred-and-fifty dollars.

Without batting an eye he announced he would take them. His wife, also without hesitation, took the bowl.

It was such unexpected windfalls that made it possible for me to keep going. I did quite well after an exhibition where a couple had seen some cups they liked. They came to the studio and bought six of them, but as I was packing them up they remarked that they seemed paler than the ones in the show.

"By 1950 Beatrice was beginning to create extraordinary luster surfaces. In fact, the works were so unique that there is no real comparison that can be made within the ceramic tradition. In aesthetic terms the work resembled most closely the exquisite glass antiquities of Egypt with their lustrous patina (the result of centuries of being buried) . . . A luster glaze is a surface which reflects light waves to produce a diffraction effect, resulting from the presence of metallic salts on the glaze surface. This is brought about through reduction firing, a technique in which the kiln is denied oxygen during a part of the firing process."— Garth Clark, art historian

"That was another set," I replied, "made especially for the exhibition. It is very expensive so I put it aside."

They asked to see it.

The gallery had priced the tea set at fifteen hundred dollars, for it had a rare iridescent glaze. I brought it out of the storage area. I did not have the nerve to ask so much money, so I mumbled twelve hundred dollars and made a move to take it away.

"Twelve hundred. We'll buy it." In addition they walked off with a figure and several gold lustre bowls.

One of the nicest sales I ever made was to a dignified man who announced upon arriving, "I have one shelf full of pottery that is five thousand years old and another of pottery one thousand years old. The third shelf is to be modern pottery and I want all of it to be yours."

On another occasion a young man from New York arrived at my studio. They were opening an elegant tearoom and wanted to carry my work. I suggested that he might want to carry a less expensive line, but he insisted.

"But do you know how to run a business?" I asked with maternal concern. "Do you have sufficient financial backing to carry you for several months?"

He grinned while I lectured like a wise old hen. Thoroughly enjoying himself, he stayed an hour and signed my guest book as he left. Later, I glanced at the name: Whitelaw Reid. No wonder he smiled—the Reids possessed one of the truly big American fortunes; he could afford to have anything he wanted for his tearoom.

I love to do bordellos. I realize the reason I do is that they are a release from my shock over discovering Roché had slept with so many women. Even though I'd read Dostoevsky and Tolstoy, I never dreamed such a thing existed in the world. It was a great shock. I still haven't gotten over it.

One time five handsome young airline executives walked into my studio and announced: "We have decided we want you to make Christmas presents for our staff. We want forty ashtrays."

"I'm not in the ashtray business."

"We're offering you five hundred dollars."

"I do not like to reproduce. Your order is not unappreciated, but during the time it takes me to make forty ashtrays I could make three lustre bowls of beauty, which would sell for two hundred dollars each. Much less effort, much more beauty."

They were clearly amused. Here was a little artist—they did not know how poverty stricken—refusing their magnificent offer.

We argued for more than an hour, in fun. Finally the most persistent of the men so enchanted me with his masculinity that I gasped, "You've won! I will make your nasty order, not because I want it, but because I like you."

"It's a deal. Now you are to put an 'M' in the middle of each ashtray."

"An 'M!'"

The deal was off, and all the masculine charm in the world could not convince me otherwise. The next day I went to the bank and borrowed four hundred dollars for dental work.

Several times a doctor and his wife came and bought bowls. One afternoon they appeared and the young wife was wearing a beautiful ring her husband had just given her. My suspicious mind wondered whether a guilty conscience was involved. After she bought a bowl I went into my workroom to package it. Her husband followed.

While I wrapped the box in metallic blue paper he asked: "How is it you do not have a boyfriend? I have been here several times and I have never seen one."

"A man must be special to interest me," I said, tying the box in pink ribbon. "He must have sensitivity, humor, and imagination."

His brown eyes grew larger and were about to melt down over his face when he drawled with tremolo: "I have sensitivity, humor, and imagination." There was silence, a good black silence. I thought of his young wife within earshot and answered: "You know, I am writing a book . . . and this is what I call it . . . 'All Men Are Bastards.'" With his chin in the air he walked out of the room.

Generally I would not take special orders. Because I used experimental methods, it was impossible to guarantee effects. One day a millionaire approached me about doing a tile composition for his patio. He wanted a cowboy on a horse chasing a buffalo. I had never done a cowboy on a horse chasing a buffalo, and never wanted to. But the millionaire was charming and charm is my Waterloo. I accepted his order. For four days I prepared various sketches. When the man saw them he drawled: "I guess the horse is all right, but the buffalo is not realistic."

My eyebrows lifted. I had copied the buffalo from a photograph.

"Do you mind if I take this drawing to an artist friend and have him do a buffalo that is more realistic?" he inquired.

Not wanting to be temperamental, I consented. When he came back the buffalo was indeed changed, and so was the horse and cowboy. I forced myself to say politely: "This is not my composition. I cannot do it."

He implored me and, reluctant to disappoint, I weakened. "I will put this drawing on tiles for you, just to please you, but I will not sign it." That night in bed, the nightmare of a cowboy on a horse chasing a buffalo pursued me. I had

July 1984

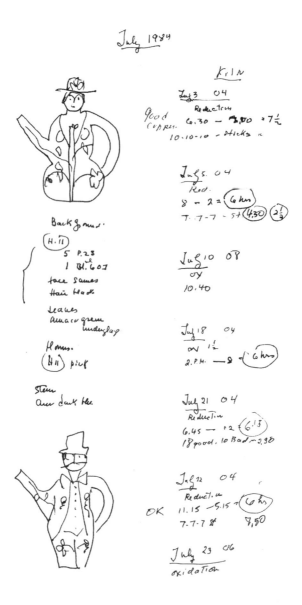

Kiln

July 3   04
Reduction
Good
Copper   6.30 — 3.00 = 7½
10.10.10 - sticks

July 5. 04
Red.
8 - 2 = (6 hrs)
7. 7-7 - 5+ (4.30) (2½)

July 10   08
oy
10.40

July 18   04
ov 1½
2.P.M. — 8 (6 hrs)

July 21   04
Reduction
6.45 — +2 (6.15)
18 good. 10 Bad — 9.30

July 22   04
Reduction
OK   11.15 — 5.15 (6 hrs)
7.7-7 8+   7.50

July 23   06
oxidation

Background:
(H.11)
5 P.23
1 Bl.607
face Sames
Hair black

Leaues
Amaco green
underglaz

Flowers.
(H11) pink

Stem
Amaco dark tan.

I am not a chemist. I experiment with glaze formulas, usually using the unpredictable reduction firing, when the kiln is smoked. I keep records of every piece made, and though effects cannot be duplicated, the records are stepping stones to new experiments. Rarely am I pleased with the results, but I keep on trying and that is important. Only in action do we discover what is wrong or right. Edison, the great inventor of the electric bulb, when consoled on having made ten thousand experiments, replied the time had not been wasted, because he had learned what he did not want. If the sea offers no challenge the navigator cannot learn to sail.

gone against my principles, for an artist should only do his or her own work. I mailed back the sketch.

When I heard that the editor of *House Beautiful* was coming to visit my place, I began rearranging and putting everything in order. Only two visitors appeared while the shelves were pulled apart, but they left after a few minutes. Never had the exhibition room been more impressive than it was the next day. And no one appeared! In the evening I phoned to check about what happened and was informed: "But they did visit your place."

"They did not. I was in all day and only two people came in while I was busy cleaning."

"That was they."

Live and learn.

Never in my right mind did I think I would end up running the place myself. I thought anyone had a better business sense. But while I do not have a commercial mind, in other ways I am business-like. I pay bills promptly, am punctual, my word is my bond, and I am so organized I could be a planet around the sun. After years of hoping someone else would manage my place, I finally accepted the responsibility, consoling myself that people are more important than pots.

Pottery for me is not a pursuit of glory, but a daily discipline of pursuing accuracy. In India it would be called my dharma. Life is dual. There is matter and spirit, and one cannot function completely without the other. For creativity, the spirit side, to work, the matter side must be strong enough to hold the spirit side. If the form has cracks, the spirit leaks.

The Arensbergs Die

Over the years Walter and Lou had grown to like Steve, and we had drifted back into each other's lives. After I moved to Ojai, Lou and Walter phoned me once a week, and Lou frequently came to the house with friends.

Lou wanted to move to Ojai, and Walter dreamed of driving through the streets lined with orange groves, but he never felt well enough to make the trip.

In the early fifties Walter had several operations. Lou did not like being alone in the big house in Los Angeles and asked me to stay with her. It was scary for two women alone in a big house, isolated far from neighbors. Even though my bedroom was filled with consoling art treasures—a Duchamp and a Rousseau—and a genuine early American bed in which to sleep, being there gave me the creeps.

After Walter was released, I myself had to go into the hospital for several weeks with minor surgery and both Lou and Walter were lovingly concerned, phoning me every day. Two weeks after I came home Walter phoned. He had difficulty speaking. He told me that Lou was ill and had just been given a blood transfusion. I was shocked. In their concern for my health not one word had been said about hers. Three days later he phoned again; Lou had cancer.

During the next three weeks we were constantly in touch. Lou regained some of her lost weight and we pretended that all was well. Then Lou had to return to the hospital. Walter was almost out of his mind; he phoned continually and I tried to console him, knowing there was really no consolation. On November 24, 1953, Lou died.

It was a week before Walter was able to speak with me. He told me he was lost, that he did not know how to function or what to do with himself. "She was such a wonderful woman, so kind, so generous. You cannot know how generous she was." I begged him to let me come stay nearby for a day or two, but he would not hear of it. I suspected he was drinking and did not want me to know—for years Lou had tried to restrain his drinking. Some days he called me two, three times, his voice desolate and his speech incomprehensible. Over and over again he murmured how much he loved Lou, how completely he had depended on her. He said he had never bought a painting without first consulting her.

Finally he agreed I could come and spend a night with him after the opening of my exhibition at the DeYoung Museum in San Francisco. The Wednesday before, he rang up in a forsaken voice. "I cannot see you. I am in no condition to see anyone."

The next day, two months after Lou, he died. He was all alone in the big house, with his fabulous treasures that had become meaningless to him. He did not want to live without Lou.

Part of me died too when they both left. For years they had been my family. Their friendship had sustained me through my darkest periods. Not only had we met on the daily little things, but they opened my eyes to the vast world of art; it was a privilege to be in their home. Their friendship had done a great deal in forming me as an artist. My work would have lost a certain quality had I not known them. I never attend a museum exhibition where I do not think of them.

Marcel had been in California the year before and visited me in Ojai with Helen Freeman and Lou. He was delighted with the house and inspected the building, the garden, the rock walls. Knowing Steve's resistance to the move, he kept telling me how wise I was to choose Ojai. The memory of our close friendship struck me with sad intensity and it had been hard to say goodbye. Then I wrote to him in New York about Walter. He wrote back:

> Thank you for your sweet letter telling me of Walter's death. It is hard for me to accept that he went so quickly . . .
>
> Philadelphia is preparing the opening of the Arensberg collection for October, and I go there from time to time to make sure that the presentation is the best possible.
>
> Also, I married Teeny Matisse, ex-wife of Pierre Matisse (The Gallery). I am enchanted with this change in my life. I was operated on for appendicitis in Cincinnati, where we were spending a few days. The operation was followed by pneumonia, and I have just returned to New York practically all right.
>
> In a month I leave for Cincinnati for a prostate operation.
>
> You see, a busy year. I obtained my citizenship papers and am awaiting the final OK to be declared an American citizen.
>
> Give my warm greetings to Helen Freeman to whom I owe several letters.
>
> I am happy to know that you enjoy your work so much.
>
> Affectionately,
>
> Marcel
>
> (Translated from the French)

Later, en route to Europe, I went to see the Arensberg collection at the Philadelphia Museum of Art. Originally the entire collection had been given to the University of California in Los Angeles, with the understanding that the university would put up a new building to house the collection intact. When a medical center was built instead Lou and Walter asked for the collection back. Fiske Kimball, director of the Philadelphia Museum, offered to devote an entire wing of that museum to the Arensberg Collection, so Walter and Lou agreed to let their works go there.

When I saw the collection I was crushed. After the vitality of their home, the cold, impersonal display felt like a tomb. Kimball had a reputation for bewitching collectors, but not for his love of modern art; he recognized a good value for the museum. Subsequent visits to Philadelphia, however, put my mind at ease. Then Curator of Twentieth Century Art (she is now the Director) Anne d'Harnoncourt redesigned the installation and the pieces now look beautiful.

After Philadelphia I stopped in New York to see Marcel and his new wife, Teeny, then went on to France to visit Roché. Roché lived in Paris with his wife, Denise, and had by now written *Jules et Jim*, the novel which Francois Truffaut would later make into a film with Jeanne Morceau, Oskar Werner, and Henri Serre. Because the story concerns two young men who are close friends and a woman who loves them both, people have wondered how much was based on Roché, Marcel, and me. I cannot say what memories or episodes inspired Roché, but the characters bare only passing resemblance to those of us in real life!

Roché and I had remained in touch, writing to one another three or four times a year. Through the years I wrote him about everything: Steve, Rosalind, Krishnamurti, and my new house. Occasionally I discoursed on art:

Ojai, 1937

Most painters are too clever. They are concerned with methods and form, and reveal little of birth and true freshness of approach. So much of art is from the mind, and not the heart. I do not refer to Marcel, Picasso, the few great, but to the many very talented who are so clever. Marcel is an intellectual painter, yet he has "birth" and feels the pain of true creation. I wonder if art should not be anonymous, then a lot of the nonsense of collectors would be done away with. It is the objet d' art, and not the artist that matters.

. . . or other matters of the heart and soul:

Ojai, 1937

There are times I regret so many years of celibacy, then am attracted to some man and would like to roll and roll and hug and hug. But generally that state of mind does not bother me and I am sublimated in my work. That which is the finer part of me realizes that consciousness itself is sex, creative, and that if one pours oneself vividly into the life around, the frustration of mere physical desire is dissolved.

In 1938, when he decided he wanted a son and made a deal with his former mistress to marry her if she would bear his child, he wrote:

Please do send me good snapshots of Marcel in Hollywood. I am so glad you have seen him there and I wonder if he would come for a longer stay and make some money in connection with modern film in Hollywood?

I did not know I wanted a son or a daughter, and discovered it only at 51. Germaine accepted it in a way, but I suffered, to a point which has upset her natural generous balance. Yes, her fragility is responsible—and I am, too.

I shall have fresh news for you when I see Marcel in Paris, at the end of this month . . .

WIth much love, Pierre.

Later I wrote and encouraged him to bring his new family to California:

Ojai, 1939

It is superb country, open to life, joyous, growing and full of new world vitality. With effort and time you could find an unfurnished house for $25 or $30 per month. It cost me about $25 a month to run the house, and that includes lots of butter, fish, and occasional meat, fruits.

Carrots $.04 a bunch
Cauliflower .10 a head
Butter .30 a pound
Eggs .30 a dozen
Bread .10 a loaf
Milk .10 a quart

It is paradise for children, such delicious sunshine. I am not sure your wife would like it here at first, outwardly the country is crude. Once you see beneath and open up to the beauty of space, yellow hills, palm trees, one is lost. It is almost carnival, if one is not starving . . .

. . . and, as usual, I wrote about matters of a more romantic sort:

I am happy these days, in love with two men. Wish they would hug me. Both at the same time. Hug hard, always the same men. My doctor, who is old, who is busy, my pottery teacher, who is homosexual, who is busy. Have you ever known of such stupidity as mine! And I love both these men, they are fine, noble—yes, alas! They think I am noble, and that the word fornication is something a sweet middle-aged thing as myself has never heard. Oh, beautiful fornication, when one is in love.

Instead, I take care of my plants. My dear garden. I am so happy in my garden, and my workshop under the trees. When one is alive, all is fornication, because all is movement and creativity. When one sees that sex is no longer a problem, one drops it. I should call myself 'La Celibatrice au Soleil.'

After the war broke out, I received a note from him on a torn sheet of paper. It occurred to me that there must be shortages and I began sending him emergency staples, food, and clothes. Before the war ended, I had sent him more than two hundred boxes. Two examples:

Box 66: 1 broth, 1 Jello, 1 box caramels, 2 soaps, 2 small teas, 1 shirt, 1 sweater, 1 waist, 1 dress, 1 coat, 1 nightgown.

Box 67: 1 prune, 1 chocolate bar, nuts, 1 Babo soap, hand soap, 1 cooking chocolate, 1 cookie mix, 3 small Castillo soaps, 2 gray skirts, 1 sweater.

From Roché, Paris, 1949:

Please send one cartridge for my Eversharp. Yes, we have sugar left.

Please 2 more 'Miracle Cements.' Also, please some more big airmail envelopes.

Some early works of Marcel have been discovered at his brother's, Jacques Villon. If Walter buys any you will see them. They are temporarily in my place and you would, no doubt, enjoy them as much as I do.

My son beats me often at chess. Marcel has given him lessons. Pity some of your surrealistic pottery is not included in Walter's collection. Shall I tell Marcel?

He wrote in 1950, finally ending a ritual that had lasted nearly a decade:

It is a relief for you not to have to send any more rice, sugar, oil—but a still greater relief for us to be able to do without asking you any more for those things.

Marcel and I are going to have dinner together tonight and I shall write you more tomorrow. Three museums, Whitney Modern Art, New York and Boston, have issued a common statement on Modern Art. Interesting, the Societe Anonyme of Marcel has published its own catalogue with many photos and notes by Marcel, only on the important creative artists.

Marcel is sleeping for a few days in my Paris home. I had not seen him since 1946. He is thin and always delightful. He is sure of your success and admires you. It is through him that I have known you!

Our loves,

Pierre

I wrote back:

If you come here you would probably quickly make friends. It is really a new world, this California . . . and I am crazy about it. It has magnificent space. The men have wonderful ideas for architecture, are masculine and lose no time going after what they want. There was a cowboy chasing me. Suddenly the other day he threw his two arms around me, held me tight and cried in front of a passersby: 'If you do not permit me to kiss you in private, then I will kiss you in public.' And he kissed me several times. I liked that . . ."

I See Roché Again

My beloved Roché had become a sweet old dodo.

I finally had some extra money and was thinking of flying to Peru. I longed to see their textiles and gold ornaments. But when I learned Roché was unwell, I decided to go to France to see him. Now a semi-invalid, he was not strong enough to meet me at the airport in Paris, so Denise came in his place. Though she and I had never met, the moment we set eyes on one another we got along. In typical French manner, I was accepted as part of an erotic past; mistresses are taken for granted in French married life. We all knew there was nothing deader than dead love.

Roché was more handsome than I had remembered him. His face, with its high cheekbones and long lines, had great character. His son, by this time in his late twenties, was good-looking and vigorous, and if I had mischief in mind, it would have been for the son rather than the father! My darling Roché, who had once broken my heart, had become a sweet old dodo. Roché spent hours on the phone, but no one was invited and no one dropped by, even though their two-story home in the Parisian suburb of Sevres was full of Picassos and Brancusis.

Miro and Artigas were holding a ceramic exhibition in Paris and their approach to glazes amazed me with its free technique. Artigas, the great ceramic technician of Spain, talked to me about lusters and kindly gave me several old Spanish formulas. Later, back home, I tried them, but they did not work out, for my glaze material, fuel, even water was different from that found in Spain. Any variation spoils a luster experiment, so subtle is the humor of a kiln. I was forced to go on with experiments on my own.

During my stay in Paris, Roché arranged for me to call on Brancusi, whom I had known in New York and had introduced to the Arensbergs. Brancusi was eighty-two, and laid up with a broken hip.

I walked through a narrow street, passing an unkempt square where refuse was piled and a dead bird lay sadly abandoned. I came to a low building, saw his name painted on the door, and knocked. No one answered—I waited, and then resolutely turned the knob and entered.

I found myself in a large, high-ceilinged room, filled with tables and chairs which Brancusi had carved. Brancusi was on a narrow couch in one corner of this studio; except for some grey in his beard he seemed little changed. We talked of temples, gurus, and magic, for he was deeply involved with Eastern philosophy and life.

He said, "Art today is without depth. It is born of intellect, or skill, without any spark from the soul of man."

"I love Rousseau," I said.

"Ah, there was a man who painted from the heart. He towers above the fakers of today for all they do is caca." He repeated the word with relish.

He settled into his cushion, took some pills, and laid tranquilly gazing beyond me. Unable to relax in the silence, I prattled on: "Art is like music, the eye as well as the ear gets trained. It took me fifteen years to understand Miro."

With a faraway light in his eyes he muttered morosely, "If one is free of self, one comes into a great consciousness, a comprehension beyond that of most men. I have done nothing that matters, but in the great consciousness I create beautiful things. I cannot bring them down from there to here. *Je nage dans la misere*." His head dropped and he repeated, as if to himself: "I drown in misery."

"Do you fear death?" I asked, deciding he wanted to talk only about serious subjects.

"No," he muttered. "One does not know when one dies."

"I too am convinced one does not know when it happens."

"Life and death are the same," Brancusi pointed out emphatically, "just different vibrations. There are rays we do not see, but know exist, so there are vibrations of being man cannot reach."

"One hears impressive things about life after death, but I know not whether they are true."

"I know however that they are!" His eyes flashed. "For I died as a child. I drowned when I was a boy. All my life passed by me, I knew I was dying, and as death touched me, my feet touched ground. I was jumping from one vibration to another. I came out of the ocean, belching water like a fountain. I knew I had died, and that I had been allowed to come back."

He lifted his face to listen to the patter of rain on the roof. Then, with a certain difficulty, he reached for a rope near his couch, and pulled and closed a skylight. "We are in the deluge again. When this deluge gets worse, nothing will be left. My work will be gone."

"You may be mistaken," I consoled. Standing, I turned toward his marble bird in space, soaring into the unknown. Transported by its beauty, the bird was already off this earth. I came back to the couch and took Brancusi's hand in mine; it was warm—his eyes too were warm and guileless like a child's. We did not say anything further, not even goodbye. I just walked out the door.

When Denise and Roché left for the south of France, I proceded on to Spain to see the marvelous primitive wooden statues in the Catalonian Museum. Ignored by tourists, it is truly one of the great museums of the world. I chose cheap hotels and restaurants and saved my money to buy folk art. In joyous spirits, I spent my time roaming museums and churches and passed hours at the Prado in front of the paintings by Velazquez.

While in Spain, I received a remarkable letter from Roché. Although his wife was a jealous woman, he told me, she had liked me so much she wanted me to come and stay with them in the south of France. She offered to give up her bed in their bedroom and sleep in the bed in the hallway so that Roché and I could talk early in the morning. This generous suggestion revealed her true love for Roché, whose happiness was her first consideration. However, I had already enjoyed several weeks with them and longed to see Portugal. Besides, I had made it a rule never to flirt with a married man. Together again—in the same bedroom—I couldn't take a chance!

Because I had to watch my funds carefully, I took a three-day bus ride to Portugal instead of flying. The first night the bus stopped at a splendid hotel with marble halls and bellboys in uniform. I waited to be directed to third-class quarters; my ticket did not qualify me for luxury.

To my surprise, I was led to a gorgeous room with an enormous bath and working plumbing. At dinner everyone appeared in evening dress except me, a fresh scarf being my only change of costume. The second night we were billeted in a palace. I realized they had inadvertently put me in a first-class group, and since the mistake was not my doing, I decided to accept my good fortune.

At dinner an orchestra played and beautiful women chatted in low-necked gowns with powdered bosoms heaving in time to the music. An impressive maître d' led me, in my shameless tailored suit, to a table, where in solitary splendor sat a perfectly groomed Englishman, every hair on his chest in place.

Fish was passed, but I did not take it. I saw his eyebrows rise. Meat was passed and I did not take that either. His eyebrows raised a second time and he scowled: "What nonsense is this, not eating meat? I raise sheep." "Isn't the music wonderful," I said, changing the subject.

After dinner we sauntered into the sitting room, where I hoped for an evening of gentle flirtation. There were magazines on the table and, wanting to impress him with my erudition, I picked up *The Saturday Review*. "I love political articles . . ." A lie, if ever I told one. I caught myself in a mirror and saw my hair hanging in disarray, a hairpin falling out of it. Turning, I saw him disappear through the door.

The next morning a formidable concierge came up to me in a threatening manner. "Madame, we have a phone call from Madrid. You do not belong in this hotel. There has been a mistake, you have to leave. We are returning you to where you started."

The proper Britisher was standing in a corner watching, his tight mouth loosened into a smirk. I answered, "You are not going to stop me from going to Portugal. I have my ticket."

"Madame, we are sending you back to Madrid on the next bus."

For once I was ready to fight; in good faith I had paid for a ticket, and whatever mistake had been made, it was not of my doing. In an equally threatening tone I said, "If you make trouble for me I will get in touch with the American ambassador."

The porter flinched as I marched back on the bus. I visited Toledo and saw the Cathedral's Museum, with its magnificent vestments embroidered in emeralds, rubies, and diamonds. The entire time the Britisher stood behind me, watching as if I were going to steal them.

That evening we arrived in Lisbon, and I was the first to get off. The Britisher was sitting in smug frigidity in the back of the bus. Pausing at the door, with one foot on the steps, I lifted an arm, waved, threw him a kiss, and cried out, "Goodbye, darling. I will never forget the night we spent together," and quickly jumped off while the ladies gasped in astonishment.

If I loved Spain, how can I express my feelings about Portugal, which I loved even more? My room was a delight. The plumbing worked and there were no cockroaches. I went to marvelous museums, saw incredible jewels, unbelievable antique shops, and ate desserts of exquisite sweetness and abundance.

When it was time to return to America, I had just enough money left to pay the hotel, tips, and cab fare to the airport, but not enough for extra luggage, of which I had a considerable excess. My suitcases were crammed with old dolls, silver, ornaments, as well as a painting weighing at least twenty pounds. I could not bear to part with anything, though I feared I might be forced to when my baggage was weighed.

It was a beautiful, sunny morning when I arrived at the airport, but my heart sank as I entered: the only hard-faced man I had seen in all of Portugal stood at the scales. Which of my treasures would he make me leave behind? He weighed my luggage and the heavy painting.

"First class?"

"No." I stood waiting for the axe to fall.

"Tourist?" he roared.

"Si," I answered bleakly.

He picked up my grips, strode to my side, leaned over, and breathed into my face: "Here, take these with you. Don't say a word. Walk to the plane, take your seat, and be silent. . . You have thirty-eight dollars overweight."

As if in a trance I passed through the gate. I had thirty-two dollars left in my purse.

More Transitions

Rosalind Rajagopal

After three months in Europe, I returned to Ojai and resumed my pottery and teaching at the Happy Valley School. I continued to sell my pots and have exhibitions in Hawaii at the Honolulu Academy of Art, and at the Santa Barbara Museum. There was also one at the Contemporary Craft Museum in New York, which I could not attend because of Steve's deteriorating health.

He had become more irritable—if that was possible—more deaf, and now even more blind. Unexpectedly, I had to contend with health problems of my own: a tumor was discovered on my kidney and the doctor believed it might be cancer. "All right," I said to him, "we will make a date for surgery immediately. If you find cancer, don't keep me lingering. I want to go as quickly as possible. I have no fear."

I arranged to be operated on following the opening of my exhibition at the Pasadena Museum and went through the next three weeks certain my end was near. I told no one except Rosalind. She had a right to know, since a new teacher would have to be found to teach pottery at the school.

Facing death, I appreciated having time to put affairs in order. I went to the opening of the exhibition, to a party in my honor afterward, and decided it was a wonderful way to go!

Coming out of the anesthetic, I heard Rosalind tell me everything was all right. There was no cancer and they had left in my kidney. Drifting into consciousness, I wearily found myself thinking, "Now I must go back to all the bother of living . . . oh, dear."

I soon recovered and was back in my workroom, busy as ever at my wheel and kiln. But as we grow older, the real drawback to surviving is having to endure the loss of others.

I received a cable from Denise telling me that Roché had died. His death left a void; his love was paternal, yet he taught me that the physical relationship between a man and woman is natural and beautiful.

A letter from Denise followed her cable:

> April 20, 1959
> . . . I hold many regrets for him, always about happy things which he can no longer enjoy. The good letters from his friends, the sun rising, the lilacs and the flowers, etc. The house is still full of his presence and joy of living, and I cannot be sad. It is like a big force vibrating around us.
>
> Pierre did not realize he was dying, because he was carried away in a short time. Two days before, he had a rather violent gastric attack, but he rallied from it. The morning that he died he made several telephone calls. He was cremated, as he wished, at Pere Lachaise . . .
>
> . . . Marcel Duchamp is in Spain. He knows, and I have received a letter full of heart from him. He was the only masculine friend that Pierre had.
>
> I kiss you tenderly, Beatrice
> Denise
> (Translated from the French)

From Marcel in Spain, I received the following letter:

> Thank you for your letter, full of sadness, shared by all of us. I received a long letter from Denise, giving me a long description of Pierre's last moments. We left from New York for Lisbon the 9th of April, and he died the 9th of April in the afternoon. We only heard the news when arriving in Spain. We have been here for two months and soon leave for Paris. We have given up our New York apartment and have no address in the United States.
>
> Happy to know you are working with joy and profit.
> Affectionately from all of us,
> Marcel

Over the next several years Steve continued to fail. Eighty years old and blind in one eye, he refused to give up driving; people complained after a series of accidents. Then his good eye bothered him and he underwent surgery.

After ten days in a hospital I brought him home. He walked into his room and found he could not see anything. He was totally blind. The doctor never bothered to warn us, and with the terrible realization happening so suddenly, we did not know what to do. Steve stumbled and groped like a wild animal in frustration. Jack Case and Rhea, his second wife, again came to the rescue and found a nurse. We begged him to go to the hospital, where he would get good care, but he refused to leave.

Finally, a neighbor helped to "kidnap" him and drove him to the Veteran's Hospital on Sawtelle. Even the hospital had a problem with him. He was loud and disruptive, and his profanity astonished both the patients and staff. Nurses and doctors came from other floors to listen in amazement, for they had never heard anyone cuss the way Steve did. He really had a talent. Once in the middle of the night he got out of bed, somehow found his way to the pantry, and gorged on cold chicken and ice cream. Returning to the ward, he climbed over the beds of two sleeping patients trying to find his own bed.

The hospital could not let it happen a second time; Jack and Rhea brought him back to Ojai.

Steve insisted upon lolling in a chair at the entrance of the exhibition room where he could greet my visitors. He was stubborn and mean as a stingray. I could not handle him. Finally the doctors got him to move to a rest home. I suspect they gave him heavy doses of tranquilizers, for he hardly recognized me when I visited. He had been there only three weeks when he lapsed into a coma. I again went to hear Krishnamurti; he spoke of death and his words held consolation. That afternoon I returned to the home and sat with Steve all day.

On the evening of May 30, 1960, he died. I broke into sobs. None of my friends thought I mourned his loss, but one does not surrender a companion of twenty-seven years easily.

It was only a matter of weeks before Reginald phoned. I was prepared.

"I have a wonderful idea," he chimed. "You are lonely. I am lonely, so I will come and rent Steve's room."

"The room is rented," I half lied—a man had taken a look at the room the day before. Steve had warned me that Reginald would make a move after he was gone, and cautioned me not to weaken.

The next day Reginald wrote two letters, love letters:

July 1960
. . . You know how it has been with me all these years (ever since Steve first came to live with you). I have been bitterly, bitterly jealous of his living with you all this time . . .

Dearest B., there has been no one in my life with whom I have had the depth of love, of understanding—that I had with you. In New York we loved each other, we joined the Theosophical Society together, met Krishnamurti together. I write to tell you that I love you. I believe that you knew this all the time; you knew it when I married Frances. I want to be with you again.

All my love, R.

. . .

B. dearest. Please don't misunderstand yesterday's letter. It was, and is, utterly true. I am, at present, quite a sick man. I love you too much to want to intrude that sickness on you, but if my mental condition can improve my health, perhaps even be miraculously remedied by my restrained love for you . . . I love you . . . so . . . dearest friend of these almost 40 years! Please telephone. I see you now in your beautiful garden; it is the only place where I have felt at home all these last years. At present above all things, I need companionship. I do so need your dear friendship, such as we used to have. It was to me so Beautiful. R.

His letters did not move me. I suspected he was only trying to butter me up to get the room, but I wanted to keep in touch and immediately wrote back. He did not answer, or phone. I still had not learned.

Another Love Affair

Once again alone, it was now time to enjoy a life of solitude, stability, and quiet—or so I mistakenly thought.

One day Irene Andrews, whose husband was the writer- producer Robert Hardy Andrews, invited me to a luncheon to meet a distinguished Indian woman. Although India meant nothing to me then, I wore a spectacular turban. Opposite me at table sat a middle-aged, stern-faced Indian woman wearing a crimson sari. I smiled, but she did not smile back. I decided it was the turban.

Later Irene brought the Indian woman, Kamaladevi Chattopadyay, to my exhibition room, and as she entered she exclaimed, "This is the most beautiful pottery I have seen. We must have it in India. Would you like to come to India?"

I said "yes" to be polite and forgot all about it. I went back to work on an exhibition for the Phoenix Museum, and soon matters of even greater significance filled my life.

Rosalind phoned one morning and told me Helen Freeman had gone to a Christian Science home to relax. A cold wind compressed my heart as I recalled how pale and frail she looked the last time I had seen her.

Five days later, on Christmas, Helen was dead from breast cancer. She had been ill for thirteen years and kept up a valiant front until the end. For those of us who loved her, it was like a light going out of the world. She had done so much for each of us. It was her encouragement which started me in pottery.

Harriet von Breton, knowing my grief over Helen, drove me to Phoenix for my exhibition, where I had to lecture to a large and distinguished audience. Tired and bereft, all I could think to talk about was preparing invoices. There was a low rumble of laughter. I continued, "An invoice is the most important thing for an artist to make. No artist makes clearer ones than I do. Museums compliment me on the fact, but the director of this museum, Dr. Hinkhouse, has never said a word, even though I make wonderful little drawings to pinpoint every item." The audience laughed heartily, and afterward I was told that it was the best speech they had ever heard.

When I returned to Ojai, a letter was waiting from the US State Department. At the request of the Indian government, I was being invited to India to exhibit my work and lecture on American crafts. Eighty pieces of my pottery would be shipped by air and my salary was to be, apologetically, seven hundred dollars a month, plus first class air fare to India.

I could not imagine why I was being asked, until I remembered Kamaladevi's visit to my studio. Though she had struck me as aloof, her interest had been genuine. Evidently, she also had enough influence to arrange my visit. I was thrilled, and had no idea what I would find halfway around the world. First I would visit Hong Kong, Japan, Thailand, and finally, India!

Tokyo was alive with extraordinary vitality.

As I prepared to leave, I was aware that Rajagopal seemed constrained. For several years there had been gossip about him and an assistant, Anna Lisa Beget. She was slim, with dark hair, and had the grace of an exotic flower. Rosalind was fond of her and had no objection to their friendship. Though Rosalind loved her husband, in many ways they led separate lives. Shortly before I left for India, Rosalind told me they were getting a divorce. The world came crashing down for all of us who loved them both so much. Their break had a curious effect on me. I began wondering what it meant to live a "correct" life, and I went off to India with a strange new attitude. I was ready for any adventure, should it come.

My first impact with the East was in Hong Kong, where a baby-faced man was both my escort and tailor. He made me a beautiful coat, and treated me to a bit of Hong Kong's night life. I am sure the coat paid for it.

On to Tokyo, where I met the minister of culture. I had cleverly packed six small pieces of pottery in my suitcase to show him. In Ojai a friend advised me not to take a turquoise vase because it was not "shibui" enough. But I liked the little vase and decided to include it. Of the six pieces, it was the turquoise one the minister loved the most. Tokyo had seen plenty of "shibui"; they wanted something different.

Tokyo was alive with its extraordinary vitality. Young people crowded the streets; taxis moved with fiendish skill through the traffic. The shops were full of delectable merchandise, the museums loaded with unbelievable treasures. Seventy percent of the city was destroyed during the war, and the old part of the city was like a maze, filled with tortuous lanes ending at uncertain angles, streets and houses without numbers. Everyone carried a map.

I stayed at the International House, which was maintained primarily for scholars on cultural exchanges and Fulbright scholarships. I met engineers, lawyers, and writers of all nationalities. We marvelled at the transformation Japan had undergone. Thirty-two years earlier it had been an agricultural country; now its technical skills were second only to Germany. Noticing the effusive friendship of the Japanese for Americans, I remarked to a lawyer, who was counsel for the American forces, that the war almost seemed completely forgotten.

The Japanese responded to what I was doing because it was what they were not doing. The only reason I was not doing Japanese pottery was that I did not know how. In my lack of technical knowledge, I pursued something that was my own.

"Overnight," he answered, then added drily: "Sex is a great democratizer. Our boys married 55,000 Japanese girls, not to mention all those who didn't bother with the legalities. You don't hate when you make love."

Japan is a paradise for American men, who find themselves in a culture that for centuries has known about sex, and happily accepted it. Like all Americans, I was curious about the Geishas. I was told they were the Japanese version of call girls, while others said they were merely highly trained entertainers. A young Japanese woman gave me a glimpse into their attitude toward Geishas.

"My father for years had a beautiful Geisha as mistress," she told me. "My mother knew nothing about it. We are a rich family; father gave mother all the money she wished, and came home every night—always after midnight. Two years ago he was dying and confessed his love for the beautiful Geisha. He asked me to look after her and a daughter he had by her years ago. I went to the Geisha, who was a lovely and wise woman of fifty, and met my half-sister. We discussed her education and decided to send her to America, for there was no chance of finding a husband in Japan without a dowry."

My last days in Tokyo were like falling in love after marriage. I became part of the pulse of the city. After my initial terror of wild taxi drivers subsided, I recognized that they were gentle young men who kept flowers in their cars and tried to help me understand the currency when they gave me change. I am sure none cheated me. On one ride, the taxi bumped into the next car; when my driver saw that no damage was done he jumped out and embraced the other driver.

Kamaladevi was chairman of the All-India Handicrafts Board and had been close to Gandhi and Nehru.

I loved to roam the Takishamaya department store where an exhibition of my work was being held. Kyoto Kusuda, an exquisite beauty who stepped out of feudal Japan to take up painting and become a modern woman, shared the exhibit with me.

I met a noted Japanese architect whose father had been right-hand man to Frank Lloyd Wright when they built the famous Imperial Palace Hotel. We were joined that evening by his lovely wife and their captivating child, with black hair and apple-red cheeks. After dinner we wandered into a movie show; *Hiroshima Mon Amour* was playing. The film showed the lovely green country, the lush hills, the curving lines of the sea, and the bomb dropping. The baby on my lap moved and kissed me. The architect turned and said, "My wife saw the bomb. She was a child and watched the cloud mushroom into the sky."

I sat there in silence with tears falling down my cheeks.

At the end of the week, I took the express to Kyoto, then went on to Bangkok. Amidst water buffalo and women working in the streets as laborers, I felt that I had finally reached a distant and foreign culture. I took a boat up the river to the Floating Market and marvelled as we passed barges of ancient design laden with vegetables and fruits, houses perched on stilts above the water with rooms open to the warm weather, and men and women sitting, talking, and eating for all to view. It was truly the river of life, both a recreation and sewer.

I decided that perhaps illiteracy worked. These people were content to live without going through analysis, watching television, or reading detective stories. It occurred to me that illiteracy might be an important way of life. I was musing on this thought as my plane touched down in India.

I walked through the airport, astonished to see women in crimson and green saris and old men with heads shaved, just a wisp of ponytail sticking out in back. The strangeness so stimulated my attention, it did not occur to me that no one had come to meet me. Three days earlier, I had sent a cable to the American Embassy, announcing my arrival, but it had not been delivered. This was India!

When I finally met Kamaladevi, I was ushered into her office and once again found her as unresponsive as a sphinx. Taken aback, I made up my mind that I would not put up with such coldness. The second time I saw her I threw my arms around her, held her tight, and told her how grateful I was for what she had done for me. She melted, and from that moment became my friend. I soon discovered that she was a truly remarkable person. She was chairperson of

Overcoming my shyness.

the All-India Handicrafts Board and, with other notable Indians, had gone to prison for the freedom struggle, defying British rule. She was close to Gandhi in his non-violent movement, and also close to Nehru. She refused honors, ambassadorships, and governorships, and maintained an independence which allowed her to act in any cause that she considered right and honorable.

ALL INDIA HANDICRAFTS BOARD AND THE UNITED STATES INFORMATION SERVICE
CONDUCT

A rare and unique Ceramic Exhibition of works of
World famous Miss. Beatrice Wood

at Sir Visweswaraiah Industrial Museum, from 2-1-62 to 7-1-62
from 10 a.m. to 1 p.m. and 4 to 8 p.m. daily,

The works of Miss Beatrice wood is well-known in the United States. The highly decorative expressionism and plastic freedom of her forms (both in glaze sculpture and pottery and especially her world famous glazes breathtaking in colour with a transparent 'precious stone' appearance have brought her well-deserved fame. Many of her great works are museum pieces and adorn the homes of the rich and discriminating.

First drawn to pottery through lustre ware, she has mastered the techniques of glaze and lustre after twenty years of experimentation. Her glazing is irregular but artfully so. The relief decorations speak eloquently of manual effort and skill and each piece has its own marked individuality making it completely different from the others. Even the clay she finds herself. She has managed to make the ancient art of pottery a modern art which is both functional and rare.

In her work Miss Wood shows a dominant spirit of adventure and experimentation with glazes, texture and shapes and her distinctive lustres offer infinite variation in colour. Muted somber colours characterise her urns and jars that have a porous texture and pitted look of antiquity.

Miss Wood was born in well-to-do American family and was reared in luxury. All this she gave up to seek a career in the world of the arts. For a while she played various roles on the stage and took up Russian Ballet. It was her acquaintance with great painters, especially the surrealist painter Marcel Duchamp that placed her on the road to this career.

The Exhibition of her works is being organised in India by the All India Handicrafts Board as part of its programme of exhibitions to bring various crafts to the notice of craftsmen and the general public.

CENTRAL HANDICRAFTS DEVELOPMENT CENTRE, No. 6, ULSOOR ROAD, BANGALORE-8.

My itinerary included all the large cities in India.

Governor Sri Prakasa of Bombay attended the opening of my exhibition, January 1962.

Working through the United States Information Service, the All-India Handicraft Board arranged for an exhibition of my pottery in fourteen cities. To my consternation, however, I found out that each city had an official inauguration at which I was expected to make a speech.

Not only did I know nothing of protocol, but I was shy. I was also accustomed to saying any mischievous, naughty remark that came to mind. I resolved to be myself and greeted everyone with spontaneous informality. Thousands attended the lectures and exhibits, and I met hundreds of people, from dignitaries to merchants and scientists. It was upon meeting one particular Indian scientist that the essence of my trip changed.

He was in his sixties, well-mannered, quiet, and spoke beautiful English. I thought to myself how comforting it would be to lay my head on his shoulder. I smiled secretly at my foolishness and we went on talking. After a silence he remarked, "I feel great peace near you." I spoke to him of detachment and he was astonished that I, a Westerner, spoke in such terms.

Without question there was a pull between us. The night before I left his city, as he escorted me home from a party, he broke out in a low voice, "I have fallen in love with you." He took me to the door and walked away.

I stood behind the closed door and broke into tears. For I had fallen in love with him.

The next morning at the airport, the moment he arrived and saw my swollen eyes, he knew how I felt. He opened his arms. I flew into them and, sobbing, clung to him. Just as we found each other, I had to tear myself away from him. I was devastated.

Perhaps if we had not admitted our feelings to each other he would have slipped from my life and memory. But I had been swept off my feet and felt the emotional response of a teenager. Age makes no difference in matters of the heart. Alone, all my love was projected onto this sensitive and caring man. Grief stricken, I went through the rest of my trip with charm and laughter during the day and tears at night.

My itinerary included all the large cities of India, and everywhere the exhibits were impressively displayed. Much care and effort had been put into the project and thousands attended. In Bombay, a modern city on the

The days were kaleidoscopic in experience.

Arabian sea, I loved the view from my window, where at night I gazed down on the statue of a knight on a golden horse, illuminated by green lights. I lost myself in a dream, seeing the silhouette of small boats moving against the grey of the ocean, their lanterns waving in the breeze. What I liked least were the "caves," rows of bars in front of which stood hundreds of prostitutes, gaily bedecked in flowers and saris—most of them young girls in their teens.

I had the good fortune to be in Delhi at the same time as Krishnamurti. Speaking in a large tent with a ceiling of red and blue, he wore Eastern garb and his hair, now white, looked transparent. His words comforted me for a short while.

In the old town of Jaipur I visited ancient palaces and a museum filled with magnificent textiles and Rajput paintings. An enchanting experience was walking in a far-off village where I saw gentle people working on a dirt road, cows sitting peacefully to the side, and a smiling pig crossing the street followed by her little piglets, which I longed to cuddle. I went into a dilapidated mud hut and watched hand-made paper being created. Outside a group of singing women came toward me and surrounded me, touching my jewelry and patting my arms. We could not exchange words, but we shared the love of necklaces and bracelets, a sufficient bond for any woman.

The last spell was a visit to a four-hundred-year-old monastery where monks still lived. Steps and pools of water led up a hill; hundreds of monkeys were leaping about and one carried her baby clinging to her belly, its tiny arms around her back, hanging just a few inches above the earth. The mystery of the past enshrouded me. I became at one with the priest with the yellow lantern, the idol with wreaths around its neck, the shrieking monkeys, and the cows.

Once back into the civilization of the city, travelling became as complicated as possible. Passports, police regulations, and transporting of pottery to the other towns consumed hours of energy. Again I wondered about the simpler tradition of illiteracy.

The days were kaleidoscopic in experience. One of my escorts took me to visit three penniless women who had left their husbands, throwing off *purdah*, the veil over their faces. They were living in such destitution that none of the officials wanted to visit them. Their faces were beautiful and strong, and they gazed at me with wonder, for they had never met a Westerner. They told me they were honored I had been willing to come and see them.

I said: "I am honored to have met you, for you had the courage to leave your husbands who were allowing you to starve, and go into the world with your children to make your own life."

I gave them each a pair of earrings and a sari, something frivolous to lift their spirits. None of them had ever owned a new piece of clothing.

I had not heard from my Indian love and had abandoned hope. It was only at the end of my trip that I once again saw the man who had so fiercely touched my heart. I returned to my hotel late one night, sad and despondent. There he was across the lobby. The telegrams he had sent were never delivered. In India this is not surprising.

Upstairs in my room we sat on the sofa, not even touching hands. We were both emotionally exhausted. He had to return in one day and my schedule was completely filled with official obligations. We dined together the next day, and even managed two hours alone in my room. I pleaded with him to stay another day, but it was impossible, just as our love was impossible. We lived thousands of miles apart. I vowed to return. He put his arms around me and I remained motionless in them. He took hold of my hand, kissed it, murmured "Darling," and was gone.

Two days later an extraordinary astrologer appeared at my door. He stood tall and mysterious, with burning eyes. "You look rich, but you are not rich. There is a man very much in your life."

Wanting to hide my grief, I drew back, "No, no, no! There is no man."

"Yes, there is. He depends on you in an unusual way. You have an extraordinary tie that few would understand."

He went on. "You will see more of each other. Your stars are full of luck." I was certain I would return to India, not only to pursue my love, but to photo-

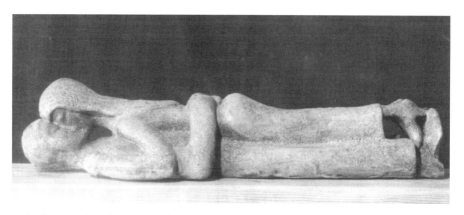

Nobody can judge what goes on between two people. If one can be compassionate, understanding, and patient, then the song of the stars begins and love is born.

graph and document the extraordinary Indian crafts I had also come to love. This was something I could do for India, in exchange for all the warmth and affection it had given me.

I returned to Delhi and had luncheon with Krishnamurti at the home of Kitty Shiva Rao, a Viennese woman married to an Indian member of parliament. Krishnamurti lifted his hands in horror at the collection of jewelry I wore. He was aghast when I told him that if I were younger I would put a diamond in my nose. Though I longed to speak with him seriously, our conversation hovered over the vanity of women.

I spent my last several days in India with Rukmini Devi at her beautiful two-story house in the one-hundred-acre compound of the Theosophical Society. Married to George Arundale since she was sixteen years old, Rukmini had done a great deal to enrich her country's artistic and cultural life. She saved the nation's art form, the dance, from virtual extinction and repopularized the weaving of old designs in saris. She was a member of parliament, active in animal welfare, and founded the Kalakshetra School in Adyar for the study of dance and textiles. Despite the mock scolding of the director of her school, we stayed up every night chatting and gossiping until midnight.

The night before I was to leave India I was desolate. While packing, my Indian love telephoned long distance to wish me goodbye. "Darling, I want you to be happy . . ." I wanted to jump into the phone, pull out every word, and cling to it, yet the connection was so poor I hardly understood what he was saying. The next morning at five a.m., when I arrived at the airport, a telegram was waiting for me. "Love, darling. Be happy."

Oh, the terrible agony of walking to the plane, going up the steps, allowing myself to be taken farther and farther away from him. Despite the great success of my visit to India, all I could do was weep in sadness.

Forlorn in America

I returned home ill from physical and emotional exhaustion. Though I was in America, my heart remained in India.

I began lecturing on India at museums and colleges, and encouraged everyone to go there. The State Department flew me to Washington, where I reported on my trip to India. They commended my efforts and said I had gone beyond my duty as a cultural specialist. Indeed. For the next four years, the high point of each day revolved around the local post office. When his letters came, I glowed. Torn as I was about this long distance relationship, I wrote Krishnamurti, hoping he would ease the weight of my pain. His answer puzzled me. It was polite and unresponsive, as if he had not read my letter. I told Rosalind. With great hesitation, she told me that difficulties had arisen and many of his friends were concerned. This was the first time that I'd heard of the impasse in the friendship of Krishnamurti and Rajagopal. Shortly after, Rosalind flew to England to see Krishnamurti and found contradictions that upset her.

Since Krishnamurti had turned away from everything theosophical, it was understandable that he wanted to be free of any label. Now I heard, in addition, that a break had come between him and Rajagopal with considerable bitterness. Old friends knew that Krishnamurti had never wanted to have anything to do with money or lawyers, and many were astounded when accusations were made of mismanagement against Rajagopal. For forty years without salary, Rajagopal had brilliantly built up an estate of considerable value for Krishnamurti. From the beginning Rajagopal was willing to turn over the estate, but friends wanted him also to turn over his archives. This was his personal property, and years of litigation followed. I was told that lawyers and

Marcel and his wife, Teeny, visited me in California.

accountants carefully examined Rajagopal's records and found everything in perfect order. This did not surprise me, for I knew how precise he was about figures and commitments.

Many were shaken by this sad affair which set friend against friend, and so contradicted Krishnamurti's message of love and tranquility.

When a film about Krishnamurti's life was made, beginning with his childhood, and even mentioning the importance of Madame Blavatsky in the promotion of Eastern thought, not one word was said about Rajogopal or Rosalind. One of Krishnamurti's followers, who had known both since they were young, said to me, "It's monstrous . . . forty years of Krishnamurti's life has been misrepresented." The lady at his side was equally disturbed: "It is incredible, because everyone knows Rajagopal gave up his career to make Krishnamurti's teaching well known and successful. Krishnamurti had such a close relationship with Rosalind and wanted her to remain at Arya Vihara until her death. He even helped bring up her daughter, Radha!" Even among the enlightened there is not always harmony.

I saw Marcel for the last time in 1963. He and his wife Teeny came to California to attend a retrospective of his paintings at the Pasadena Museum of Art, and they came up to Ojai for a large luncheon I had in his honor. Despite the publicity and adulation, Marcel was as simple as when I first knew him, quietly amused and gentle. He died in his sleep five years later. Teeny came to see me afterward and spoke of her happiness in knowing that Marcel had gone so peacefully, after a joyous evening the night before, never knowing that he had prostate cancer.

The end was also near for another love from my younger days. I went to see Reginald when I found out he had broken his hip and was in a rest home in Los Angeles. With the help of a nurse he slowly walked toward me, and though bent over and aged, dressed in his brown tweed suit he still held distinction.

"Dear, I am so glad to see you." He clung to my hand. My indifference fell from me and my love and compassion went out to him. I felt terrible, finding him in such an environment with only his son Rupert and Anais Nin willing to call on him. Though both Rupert and I delighted in poking fun of Reginald's idiosyncracies, Rupert was also loving and patient with his father. The same devotion and care was later applied to his brilliant editing of Anais Nin's writings.

I began to write Reginald long letters and send him large assortments of sweets, which I discovered he shared with no one. Three months later I drove down to Los Angeles to visit him again. I found him noticeably deteriorated, more collapsed in structure than the last time. He asked me to sit near him on his bed while he clung fiercely to my hand. With desperation in his voice he said with passion: "You are beautiful! I love your beautiful face . . . it has not changed much . . . I have done you wrong. I know that . . . but I have always loved you . . . You do not know what it was like to see Steve near you. You must have known how jealous I was . . ." Then he laid back, closed his eyes, and mumbled: "Sex is a funny thing, isn't it. It diverts . . ." He opened his eyes, sat up ". . . but my love for you has always been with me . . ."

His emotion embarrassed me, for though I held the greatest compassion for him, love as I had experienced it years ago was long gone. It felt almost indecent to recall it and bring back a hurt I had completely discarded.

Reginald spoke of death and his fear of dying alone. I felt his despair and wanted so much to comfort him. "You know as well as I that death is not the end," I said.

Anais

"But I am so alone."

"If you feel yourself dying, call on me—I will help you all I can." Then I bent down and kissed him on the forehead. He put his arms around me, wanting to cling tight.

I received a letter from Anais Nin:

Reginald died in his sleep. Unconscious on Friday night. We went to see him, but he was gone. I am writing to you for Rupert. Reginald's ashes will be buried in England near his mother.

To turn away from death, Rupert took me to your gallery, hoping your exhibit was still there, and it was. And I was able to appreciate your incredible talent and versatility, your wit and skill.

With love and admiration,

Anais

I wrote Anais and Rupert:

I weep and still weep, with you, and I rejoice that Reginald went in his sleep.

I do not know why I weep—except that he allowed his body to go one way, his soul another. I weep that I could not do more to help him. Such a beloved person, so inwardly gentle—and so selfish. So wound within himself when it should have been otherwise.

Years ago a very wise friend told me not to worry, that this life seemed to be one in which Reginald would just putter away, and that it was not his 'fate' to accomplish his heart's dream. But I, like you, sensed his heights and wished he could have stayed there . . . You have been angelic to him. I hope now that he has slipped into another plane of existence, he fully realizes what you have been to him.

In 1965, Kamaladevi returned to Ojai, and I confessed to her my passion to return to India and photograph folk art.

"You would like to do that?"

"I have been dreaming about it since my first trip."

She nodded her head. "If you want to do that, I will help."

The next day I went out and bought a good camera and enrolled at the Brooks Institute in Santa Barbara for private lessons in photography. The official purpose of my second visit would be to document and record the folk art of India, fast disappearing amidst growing industrialization.

True to her word, Kamaladevi arranged for the Handicraft Board to invite me to India again, although this time I would have to pay for my air fare and hotels. But three days prior to leaving, India and China were suddenly on the brink of war. I called Kamaladevi to ask if I should give up the trip. I saw India menaced, the country demolished, my love killed—the negative mischief of my mind ran wild. Then, as quickly as war between the two countries flared up, it died down. Kamaladevi cabled me to go ahead as planned.

En route to India, I again stopped in Tokyo for a second exhibition, and also to undergo extensive acupuncture treatment with a doctor who had been recommended. I still sought relief from my neck affliction which continued to dissipate my energy and interfere with my work. For more than a month, every day, in the cold Japanese winter, I took the subway, walked narrow streets and up steep stairs, undressed, and lay on a table while a doll of an old Japanese man, not speaking a word of English, put burning needles in various spots on my back. I did not respond to the treatment. My arthritic vertebrae were jammed together after years of muscular spasm and irritation.

When I arrived in India, my love was at the airport to meet me, but because of business and family pressure we were not able to meet often. He was a traditional Indian, devoted to his elderly mother and father, and so could not bring me, a Westerner, into his home. I understood his conflict and knew he was too old to break from the cocoon that enclosed him.

In India I went to nine astrologers, and every one of them told me that I could not have luck in the house of marriage. How well I knew. Though I took many pictures of folk art, gave lectures, and successfully accomplished the official goal of my visit, the trip was ultimately another sad goodbye.

I returned to the States, but found it difficult to stay put. Soon I flew off to Peru for a World Art Conference, where I once again met Mrs. Moshe Dayan. Several years earlier she had sent me a friendship ring after a similar conference in New York. Now we resumed our friendship. I gave her a piece of pottery for her husband's collection. In addition to being Minister of Defense in Israel, Dayan was a noted anthropologist and collector of fine artifacts.

The following spring she visited me in Ojai—with bodyguard and secretary—and gave a captivating lecture at the Happy Valley School. She also convinced me to attend the next craft meeting being held in Dublin, Ireland.

Though a bad storm left our charter group of two hundred stranded all night at the London airport, Dublin was a great success. Even Kamaladevi came from India to attend. I was frequently taken for an Indian myself, having taken to wearing saris since my second trip to India. Comfortable, economic, and lovely, I have worn nothing but saris ever since!

Mrs. Moshe Dayan visited me in Ojai.

India Keeps Calling

Until 1970, I had been directly responsible for all my sales, either through orders or at my studio. I turned down gallery offers because I did not want to send pottery out on consignment. One Sunday afternoon, as I was lazily sitting on my patio, two young men arrived. They told me they had a gallery in Los Angeles and asked to carry my work. Thinking they had a small gallery and that I might possibly be helpful to them, I agreed to let them take some bowls. I soon discovered that George Zachary and John Waller owned one of the finest galleries on La Cienega Boulevard—"gallery row"—in Los Angeles.

Their appreciation was reassuring, for the kiln can be a disappointment, and I was often on the verge of giving up pottery. They agreed to promote my work, put on exhibitions, arrange museum shows, and take care of packing, invoicing, and pricing.

Their able handling of my business affairs freed me for more work; it also added a social dimension to my life that included frequent trips to Los Angeles and more contact with clients. At last I saw myself coming into my own.

In spite of this rewarding and busy life, my mind kept going back to India. Friends told me I would not be happy if I were not making pottery, but they did not know. When I am in love the man, not creative images, are my obsession. I was also eager to continue my photographic documentation of India's folk art. When Rosalind announced she was soon traveling to Rome, I elected to join her, then continue to Turkey, Israel—to visit Ruth Dayan—and on to India.

Experiencing Rome under the nurturing care and guidance of Rosalind was a nirvanic existence. We sauntered up and down the streets, watching young lovers repeatedly succumb to the most delectable temptations, and even napped blissfully on our spread-out coats in a meadow near the catacombs. Everywhere in Rome lovers were seen arm-in-arm, a fairy tale illusion of permanence. Because of my Indian love I lowered my eyes at the melting brown glances of the Italian men.

Leaving the romantic and gastronomic paradise of Rome, I flew on to Israel. Ruth Dayan had arranged a comprehensive tour of the country, whose achievements held us spellbound. We continued on to Turkey, where I was sadly disappointed in the much-touted bazaar; then I flew alone to Iran. In Tehran, without Rosalind, I suddenly felt lost. I could not make out what was being said, nor understand the ordeal of passport, customs clearance, state taxes, and all the red tape. It was as bad as Monopoly. Having given the last of my Turkish change to the taxi driver, I did not have a dollar left to pay the visitor's exit tax. The official at the desk, annoyed at my confusion and unable to endure my

200

crocodile tears, finally lifted his hands to heaven and paid the tax himself to get rid of me. Then I could not find the gate of the plane, for there were neither signs nor numbers, nor a single soul in sight who spoke English. I could have been sixteen again, I felt so ignorant and unprepared!

My wonderful escort Ram Pravesh Singh

I came down with bronchitis and took a syrup recommended by a stranger. In the morning, when I had an important audience with the minister of the interior, I awoke dizzy and ill. The syrup had morphine in it. I floated through the meeting, forcing myself to smile—probably at all the wrong remarks. Later, still half drugged, I staggered to a taxi and arrived at the airport for the flight to Afghanistan. Confused, with eyes half open, I promptly fell on the marble floor and gashed my chin.

In a disheveled state, my uncombed hair resembling a bird's nest, and with a bandage on my face, I arrived in Afghanistan where, to my dismay, a dreamily handsome cultural officer met me at the gate. With great charm, he ushered me into a car as if I were Mae West! Afghanistan was enchanting, but I was anxious to reach my final destination: India.

Still suffering from bronchitis, I arrived in India and was met at the Delhi Airport by my wonderful escort from the United States Information Service, Ram Pravesh Singh, and Steve Huyler. Steve, whose grandfather founded the Huyler candy stores, lived in Ojai. My stories about India fascinated him, and he decided he wanted to see the country for himself—an experience that led to many subsequent trips and resulted in his writing a book on Indian folk art. Both Singh and Steve were alarmed by my appearance and rushed me to the hotel.

With war between India and Pakistan pending, Kamaladevi advised me to fly to Adyar in the south, which was considered safer than Delhi. There, at the Theosophical Headquarters, I spent the next three weeks in bed, gazing out my window and recuperating. Thinking of safety, I laughed, for the American fleet was anchored only twelve miles away, and if a shot had been fired, my window was in direct line for a hit.

When I was well enough to move, Rukmini Devi again kindly invited me to her home, and I enjoyed a few wonderful weeks with her. The harmony of the house was so great with her mother, sister, and the school director near that I began to think of myself as a Dalai Lama.

The war was brief, but America, who had stood prepared to intervene, remained unpopular. Steve had stones thrown at him when he visited a village. A number of my lectures had to be cancelled.

I toured the countryside, gasping with delight as we drove by life-sized horses made of clay and sawdust standing in the meadows. Accommodations were deplorable, but it was on these trips without an official escort that I was able to take the best photographs. Though I loved the comfort and luxury of the black limousines that took me through the streets of Bombay and Calcutta, I also loved the cheap hotels with their gentle clerks and waitresses.

In Rajastan I hired a car, guide, and driver, and started off into the far country for a few days. We passed simple shrines of marvelous designs and I became delirious with joy at the arts of villagers, and also at the sight of giraffes and goats scampering at the sight of us. Though my guide had promised hotels, he did not confirm reservations, so the first night, exhausted from miles of driving, we found there were no rooms left in the local hotel. After a moment of meditation, the guide announced that he knew a girl in the village and that he would ask her to let me sleep in her house.

The young woman was away, but her uncle, a teacher, generously said I could sleep in his room, and that he and his wife would spend the night elsewhere. Later I found elsewhere meant the kitchen floor. Tired beyond speech, with no food all day except peanuts and orange pop, I longed to close my eyes. But the teacher and his wife, and his son and his son's wife, his aunts, cousins, and nieces, who had never seen an American, gathered around the bed, which filled most of the room, and started off questions in pigeon English. "Do Americans believe in God? Are all Americans rich?"

The driver appeared with a newspaper, spread it on my lap, and presented me with more soda pop, an apple, and crackers. Thus surrounded, I feasted on crumbs while the sweet family asked one question after another. There came a time when I had to ask the inevitable question, which they did not understand. Repeating it with compelling gestures, the aunt took my hand and led me down the long hall with the rest of the group following, a procession to the water closet.

The next morning, having slept in my clothes, stiff, uncombed, and unwashed, I saw three faces curiously staring at me through the window. After quick and loving goodbyes, I started off in the heat for another day of soda pop and peanuts. I am convinced that Indians have no internal organs, for they go through certain discomfort as a matter of course.

I saw my love only once. The war made it difficult to meet, and telephone conversations were a miserable disappointment. In my heart I knew, as I had known even from the beginning, that we had lives that could never merge. Feelings, strong as they were, could not overcome tradition and distance. I reminded myself of detachment—a skill I have often needed to apply but never quite mastered—and consoled myself with the thousands of wonderful slides my trips to India had produced.

New Horizons

Many years earlier, I had willed my house on McAndrews Road to the Happy Valley Foundation. One day I was asked if I would consider selling it during my lifetime and moving to the Happy Valley land in the Upper Ojai Valley. I loved my house, having designed every inch of it and nursed cactus from tiny plants into towering figures. But on account of my love for Dr. Besant and my sympathy with her plan for Happy Valley, I gulped and answered, "Yes."

I put the house on the market and three times nearly sold it, but each time the sale fell through. Just when it seemed that moving to the Upper Valley was not in the cards, Viveka Heino called from New Hampshire, asking if the house was for sale. She and Otto wanted to move back to California. Fifteen years earlier they had driven to Ojai several times to coach me on the wheel. A warm and dynamic person, Viveka was considered the finest teacher of ceramics in America, and both she and Otto built notable reputations as potters.

There is a vibration around things made with the hands and love that no machine can copy. The handmade object has a vitality of its own that no mass-produced thing can duplicate. I told the Indians to keep designing articles to please themselves, not the customers.

Soon I moved out and the Heinos moved in. Since they were potters, the place fit them like a glove. Knowing that they loved the plants as I did, and the goldfish in the pond, I did not mind leaving the place to them. I was handing my "child" over to loving parents.

While I waited for my new home to be built, I put my furniture and pottery in storage and moved to a two-room apartment in a ranch house on the Happy Valley land. The house was a duplex I shared with two other wonderful tenants: Bob Rheem and Liam O'Gallagher. They both worried that I was not eating enough and frequently invited me to dinner. They also cheerfully provided nourishment on an aesthetic level. We often talked into the night about subjects that interested us—topics usually relating to art and artists.

I should have been impatient and frustrated in this transient state, but those seven months were the happiest I had known in years. I was on the Happy Valley land, near an orchard with wild rushes and a dried up stream full of wonderful plants. The vibrations were wonderful. I could not define it, but I could feel it. Every day I walked over to watch the progress on my house, being built on a hilltop overlooking magical mountains. Adjoining my home on the hill, separated by the garages, was the Foundation House where Rosalind, being chairman of the foundation, would live. Both of us, unable to contain our impatience, moved in on May 16, 1974—roughing it several days without electricity.

After so many years of pressure, life was idyllic, full of joy and contentment. I spent hours in my workshop overlooking Topa-Topa, the magnificent mountain which takes on a wondrous deep pink glow at sunset. With dear Rosalind nearby, young people continually calling, and a comfortable bed with a good lamp for late night reading, I wanted for nothing.

The only clouds of sadness were those which someone my age comes to expect—the loss of loved ones. Anais Nin, who did so much to encourage others and who, like myself, was such a romantic, lost her battle with cancer. I recalled a letter she had once written to me and a remark I dearly treasured:

. . . Rupert sends his special love, and we think Reginald should have married you and kept you in the family. What a marvelous relative for us.

I felt the same for them. Rupert took her ashes up in a plane and, as the sun broke through the clouds, let them fall into the ocean waves.

My dear friend from childhood, Elizabeth Hapgood, also died. Certainly part of us dies when a dear friend leaves, yet we must go on giving to the stream of life. Sometimes I think back to the remark Walter Arensberg made after the flood . . . wallpaper is very important. The wallpaper of our lives— its distractions, ambitions, possessions—helps us escape from our emptiness when we find ourselves alone.

Soon after moving to the Upper Ojai, I began getting requests from museums and scholars for information about Duchamp, Roché, Picabia, Loy, the Arensbergs, and others. Having managed to survive so long, I was seen as one of the last remaining members of a pivotal generation in art history.

French television was producing documentaries on the great artists of the past, and two men flew over from Paris to interview me. I chuckled that because of my treasured early friendships I was riding on the train as an important person. I also chuckled that out of perversity I declined to tell them whether or not Marcel and I were lovers. The Smithsonian Institute asked me to donate my papers and correspondence to them, which I did. I realized that after we are dead, every word we have uttered takes on significance. Life certainly *is* Dada!

In January 1977, the French government was having an exhibition of Marcel Duchamp to celebrate the opening of their Pompidou Center in Paris. They also displayed some of Roché's manuscripts. Because of my friendship with both men, it was decided that I would fly over to Paris for the events.

Pompidou Center was controversial, and no wonder. It had shock value, with utilities painted in brilliant colors on the outside of the building, as well as on the inside ceilings. There was a sense of restless movement, recalling a Duchamp painting in the fourth dimension. Marcel's work was shown on the fifth floor and the escalator was covered with a ribbed web, giving the impression one was riding through the entrails of a caterpillar.

Francis Naumann, an art historian who inherited both Marcel's enthusiasm and support for my work.

The catalogue was a four volume affair costing fifty dollars, which sold by the thousands. One of the volumes was the last unfinished manuscript by Roché called *Victor*. "Victor" was actually Marcel; I was a character called "Patricia," and the story was about Lou Arensberg and myself. It was very nice to find myself the heroine of a novel, although the story was so distorted I hardly recognized myself.

In Paris, I visited Teeny Duchamp, who was in the hospital following a bad automobile accident. Her red hair gleamed against the white of the sheets and I was once again aware of her delicate and special charm.

To my joy, hearing that Gabrielle Buffet Picabia was still alive, I rushed over to call on her. I entered a large room full of Picabia's paintings, and at the far end sat Gabrielle, her black eyes as sparkling as they had been fifty years ago when last I saw her. She was ninety-seven years old, and though physically frail, her spirit was as young and full of fun as I remembered years back at the Arensberg's.

I visited other friends in Paris and Germany and enjoyed a truly splendid trip. But when I returned to America, I decided I would put away my travelling shoes for good. I was weary of airports, red tape, long walks, and no porters. Though I had been around the world twice, I was not a light traveler. I carried a camera, slides for lectures, boxes of vitamins, cosmetics, a purse heavy with passport, traveler's checks, love letters, pens, lipsticks, and a notebook. And then there were my purchases . . . Much as I loved adventure, part of me, approaching ninety, was ready to sell out for comfort. I loved my beloved mountains and my cozy bed with its reading light.

One day a young art historian and authority on Dada came from New York to interview me because he heard that I knew Marcel. His name was Francis Naumann, and meeting him was like finding an old friend. He was young and handsome, with a head of delicious red hair. Bright and knowledgeable, he had a mind like a ferret, never letting go of a subject until he had found what he was looking for. He asked if I could reconstruct the drawing that was shown at the famous Independents' Exhibition in 1917, "Un peu d'eau dans du savon," for the original had been lost. I did my best, and to my amazement the replica later appeared on the cover of *ARTS* magazine in a special issue devoted to the subject of New York Dada, with an article by Francis inside.

Before Francis left my house that first afternoon I casually mentioned that I had a few old drawings tucked away in a box. With excitement, he took them back with him to New York. Due to his efforts, the Philadelphia Museum of Art mounted an exhibition of my drawings in 1978. I flew East to give a lecture and see the show, and saw my early work framed and hanging on the walls. "But these are scrawls," I blurted out in front of reporters and Anne d'Harnoncourt, curator of modern art at the museum. Suddenly I recalled Marcel's remark of so many years before: "You do not know what is good or bad in what you do!" Fortunately, Francis had inherited both Marcel's enthusiasm and his support for my work.

When the museum introduced my lecture as "Fife with Dada," I was forced to say, "What is Dada about this lecture is that I know nothing about Dada. I was only in love with men connected with it, which I suppose is as near to being Dada as anything."

Following the Philadelphia exhibition, Francis arranged for another showing of my drawings at the Rosa Esman Gallery in New York. To my surprise, the works were well received. Arturo Schwarz, the noted Italian scholar of Dadaism and a renowned authority on Eastern religions, purchased five early drawings. Later, with many other works from his collection, he lent them to an exhibition in Milan entitled "L'altra meta dell'avant-guardia," translated as "The other half of the avant garde," for the exhibition was devoted to the display of more progressive works by women artists.

My good fortune with more commercial outlets for my work was to continue when Zachary and Waller closed their gallery and I was approached by Garth Clark, who was just opening his gallery in Los Angeles. He too arranged exhibitions and took over the dreadful task of pricing my pottery. Garth is a noted historian, and now a highly esteemed dealer in the world of ceramics. I am delighted to be one of the many potters he watches over. For my ninetieth birthday Garth put on a second Blindman's Ball to celebrate my incredible age, and had me carried into the room in a sequinned sedan borne by four stalwart men in black leather. Comedian Lily Tomlin, dressed as "Dali Parton," was mistress of ceremonies, and the evening went off with true eclat. I also enjoy the artistic support and friendship of Lee Waisler. An artist of boundless energy and deep personal conviction, Lee's interest in my work has served to inspire my own productivity.

At the Philadelphia Museum, 1978

Settled Down

Dr. Annie Besant said that life's difficulties are knots by which one pulls oneself up. Since I was a child, I had an awareness that my life would be difficult. There are times, even now, when I cannot believe that I do not have to worry about being hungry. But I am glad I paid the price. I wanted to know what the world was like and, rather than remain wrapped in my mother's cellophane protection, I had to go through terrible hardships. Because I was by nature hopelessly dreamy and romantic, I had to be shaken into reality. As a young girl I knew I would have to break the shell, but I had no idea how to make it happen.

Now, here I am, situated high atop a hill facing majestic Topa Topa, whose pink glow reigns over the valley. The days are filled with making pottery, answering correspondence, reading, drawing, and writing. My beloved Rosalind lives next door, still active at age eighty with work concerning the Happy Valley School, the educational center she established with Krishnamurti more than forty years ago. She is always full of wise counsel—except when she scolds me for eating so much chocolate. The truth is, I thrive on it!

I am lovingly looked after by Dana McManus, a lovely young woman, red haired and full of light. I tease her continuously, and sometimes use her as a decoy to attract handsome young men as visitors. She miraculously helps me in matters of business, cuisine, meeting the public, and seeing that my makeup is on straight. She has a natural graciousness and charm that lifts the heaviness of days, especially when things come out badly from the kiln.

I am also grateful to Ram Pravesh Singh, my able escort from India who now spends much of his time here with us in Ojai. Singh, a traditional Indian, has taken on jobs no man from the Orient would ever consider doing: he washes dishes, waters flowers, and shows a willingness to do nearly anything that comes to hand. He tells us that his village would excommunicate him if they knew he engaged in such purely domestic activities. We have been friends now for more than twenty years. The best part of our relationship is that we never agree on anything. He fights on the side of logic—I on the side of intuition. Once we have thoroughly decimated one another, we go on in affectionate friendship. If we are able to continue with such differences, then I think there can be some hope for the rest of the world.

Regardless of disagreements, people must learn to respect other points of view. Many of the worst wars in history have been religious ones, a good number based on disagreements over the portrayal of their god—a god, of course, who none of the combatants has ever seen. I have lived through two world wars and

Singh is logical. I am intuitive. We never agree. He clings to tradition; I throw tradition in the ashcan. We fight it out day after day. But in the battle, we go on in affection, and if we two can achieve this tolerance, then peace between Russia and America may be possible.

know only too well the lesson history keeps repeating: violence never ceases by violence. Each war contains the seed of another even more catastrophic engagement. We cannot make peace with our enemy if we approach him with a gun at his throat. Civilizations have been destroyed in the past. But now, with nuclear weapons, the whole planet is threatened. Why are we so blind? By not facing reality, man is destroying the wealth of the earth and training the cream of its manhood to kill people they have never met and know nothing about. Seen from a distance, it is total insanity. Fortunately millions are beginning to protest, and perhaps someday governments will heed their cry.

With few exceptions I no longer go out, for my pots need constant attention, and with visitors coming from all over the world, I would get no work done if I succumbed to social activities. Clay is demanding, and the kiln takes hours for each firing. At night I lie in bed and plan my next day of work in the studio. I imagine the bowls, chalices, and tiles I will create, as well as the naughty figures that I enjoy making, laughing at man's inevitable absurdities. My gambling instincts are satisfied by working in luster glazes, because I can never predict how they will come out. Once I believed an artist had a sacred right to be protected from distraction. But since I have managed to create a life dominated by interruptions, I now accept that these interruptions are as much a part of the creative process as formulating a glaze.

One night at dinner several years ago, Rajagopal and philosopher Alan Watts urged me to write my autobiography. But I resisted, for inevitably one becomes one's own heroine. But friends insisted and I faced the task. After all, I decided, what is life but a history of the people one has known and loved?

In a way, my life has been an upside down experience. I never made love to the men I married, and I did not marry the men I loved. I do not know if that makes me a good girl gone bad, or a bad girl gone good. All I know is that I have loved five men—and that I shock myself.

top: Beatrice Wood, *Fusion*, glazed ceramic, 12" h x 12" w x 7" d
bottom: Beatrice Wood, *Luster Chalice*, 11" h x 10" d

CHRONOLOGY

1893   Born March 3, in San Francisco. Shortly thereafter family moves to New York.

1900   At age seven leaves for Paris with mother to study in convent school.

1905   At age twelve attends Ely School, the most fashionable New York finishing school of the time.

1907   Studies at Shipley School, Bryn Mawr, Pennsylvania.

1910   Attends drawing classes at Julien Academy. Work from this period shows ". . . the determination of an untrained student, content to embrace a profession symbolizing a break from her conservative past" (Francis M. Naumann).

1911   Studies for one year at Finch School, New York.

1912   At age nineteen announces she wants to live the bohemian life of an artist and paint in Paris.

1913   Attends the premiere of the Ballet Russe, *Le sacre du printemps* (Stravinsky/Nijinsky).

1914   At the outbreak of World War I returns to the United States and joins the French Repertory Company in New York. In two years plays more than sixty roles.

1916   September 27. Through Edgard Varese meets Marcel Duchamp, who later introduces her to the New York Dada group.

        Duchamp publishes Wood's drawing in *Rogue* magazine, edited by Alan Norton.

        Meets Henri-Pierre Roché, Louise and Walter Arensberg, and other members of the New York Dada group.

1917   Exhibits shocking assemblage, *Un peu d'eau dans du savon*, in the First Exhibition of the Society of Independent Artists, Grand Central Palace, New York.

        Designs poster for Blindman's Ball.

        Contributes to first issue of *The Blindman* magazine and co-publishes second issue.

1918   January. Leaves for Montreal to accept acting engagement at the French Theatre.

1920   Returns to New York.

        Continues close friendship with Duchamp.

        Odd jobs in Greenwich Village.

1921	Walter and Louise Arensberg move to California.
1923	Joins Theosophical Society in New York.
	Meets Indian philosopher Krishnamurti; exposure to comparative religions, Eastern philosophy, and the occult.
	Visits Los Angeles for the first time. Spends summer in Los Angeles with stage director, actor, and poet Reginald Pole. Regular visitor to the city from this time on.
1928	Moves permanently to Los Angeles, where she renews friendship with the Arensbergs, and through them meets the German Expressionist collector Galka Scheyer, Mexican painter Siqueiros, and others.
1930	With actress Helen Freeman, visits Europe to hear philosopher Krishnamurti lecture at Castle Eerde in Ommen, Holland. (This trip is recorded in an elaborate typescript album, "Touching Certain Things," published in 1982, as *The Angel Who Wore Black Tights*.) Later travelled to Freiburg, in the Black Forest of Germany, to visit Elizabeth Reynolds Hapgood, wife of the author, politician, and magazine editor Norman Hapgood, where she met the Russian theatrical director Konstantin Stanislavsky. Discovers six luster plates in Holland antique store.
1933	Enrolls in ceramics class of Hollywood High School Adult Education Department, intent on creating a matching teapot for the luster plates. First exposure to working in ceramics medium.
1938	Studies ceramics with Glen Lukens at the University of Southern California.
1940	Studies ceramics with potters Gertrud and Otto Natzler.
	Exhibition at Metropolitan Museum of Art, New York, *Contemporary American Industrial Art*.
1941	Exhibition at Raymond and Raymond Galleries, Los Angeles, *Four Craftsmen of the Arts*.
1944	Exhibition at American House, New York, *Ceramics of Beatrice Wood*.
1947	Exhibition at Los Angeles County Museum of Art, Los Angeles, *California Guild*.
1948	Moves to new home and studio in Ojai, California. Becomes closely involved with the Happy Valley Foundation and its nonsectarian school founded in 1946, by Dr. Annie Besant, Aldous Huxley, Krishnamurti, and Rosalind Rajagopal. Here she develops a mature expression of her luster glazing technique.
1951	Exhibition at Honolulu Academy of Art, Hawaii, *B. Wood-Ceramics*.
1954	Moves to new studio in Ojai on McAndrew Road. Studies with Otto and Vivika Heino intermittently from 1954 to 1979.
1955	Marcel Duchamp designs the catalogue cover for her exhibition at the American Gallery, Los Angeles.

1955	Exhibition at American Gallery, Statler Center, Los Angeles, *Ceramics by Beatrice Wood.*
1959	Exhibition at the Pasadena Art Museum, *Ceramics: Beatrice Wood.*
1961–62	Visit from Kamaladevi, chairman of the All-India Handicrafts Board, and is sent to India by the US State Department at the request of the Indian government to exhibit her work and lecture on other American potters on a fourteen-city tour.
1962	February. Exhibits at the prestigious Takashimaya department store in Japan.
1963	Attends Duchamp's retrospective exhibition at the Pasadena Art Museum. Holds luncheon in Duchamp's honor at her home in Ojai.
1964–65	Traveling exhibition, *Beatrice Wood*, California Palace of the Legion of Honor, San Francisco; Santa Barbara Museum of Art.
1965	Returns to India to photograph folk art.
1972	Third visit to India. Lectures in Israel, Nepal, and Afghanistan.
1973	Traveling exhibition, *Beatrice Wood: A Retrospective.* Phoenix Art Museum, Tucson Art Center.
1974	Moves from Ojai to a new home and studio at the Happy Valley Foundation just outside Ojai.
1975	Exhibition at Delaware Art Museum, Wilmington, *Avant-Garde: Painting and Sculpture in America 1910–1925.*
1976	August 11. Francis M. Naumann interviews Wood and discovers a large number of her drawings tucked away in a box.
1977	January. Attends the opening exhibition of the Musee Nationale d'Art Modeme, Centre Georges Pompidou, Paris, retrospective exhibition of work by Marcel Duchamp.
	Summer. Elizabeth Wrigley, former secretary to Arensberg and now director of the Francis Bacon Library, leads Naumann to a volume of Shakespeare in which Arensberg had preserved fifty-three of Wood's drawings.
1978	February 17–March 26. Ceramics exhibition at Everson Museum of Art, Syracuse, New York, *Beatrice Wood: Ceramics and Drawings.*
	March 11–May 8, 1978. Exhibition at Philadelphia Museum of Art, *Life with Dada: Beatrice Wood Drawings.*
	March 16–April 23. Exhibition at Hadler Galleries, New York, *Beatrice Wood, Ceramics.*
	May 16–June 16. Exhibition at Rosa Esman Gallery, New York, *Beatrice Wood and Friends: From Dada to Deco.*
1979	Traveling exhibition through 1981, *A Century of Ceramics in the United States*, Everson Museum of Art, Syracuse; Renwick Gallery of the Smithsonian Institution, Washington, DC; Cooper-Hewitt Museum,

the Smithsonian Institution's National Museum of Design, New York, and others.

1980   April 28. Opening at the University of Northern Iowa of a two-year traveling exhibition including Wood's ceramics entitled *The Contemporary American Potter.*

November. Eight drawings and the Blindman's Ball poster included in an exhibition of the Arturo Schwartz collection at the Museo de Arte Contemporaneo de Caracas, Venezuela, entitled *Le Espiritu Dada 1915–1925.*

1981   September. One-person exhibition at the Garth Clark Gallery, Los Angeles, entitled *Beatrice Wood: A Very Private View.* Signals active return to exhibiting ceramics, includes large body of new works.

1982   *The Angel Who Wore Black Tights* is published.

A video documentary of Wood's life is produced by Lee Waisler. Exhibition at American Hand, Washington, DC, *Women's Ceramic Invitational.*

1983   February 5–March 3. Exhibition at the California State University, Fullerton, Art Gallery, *Beatrice Wood Retrospective.* Catalogue documenting the exhibition.

March 3. Dada Ball in honor of her ninetieth birthday.

1984   Exhibition at the Garth Clark Gallery, Los Angeles and New York, *Rituals of Tea.*

1985   Exhibition by Arts Council of San Francisco at San Francisco International Airport, *Animals, Animals.*

One-person exhibition, Garth Clark Gallery, Los Angeles and New York.

Exhibition at E. B. Crocker Art Museum, Sacramento, California, *Living Treasures of California.*

Exhibition at Los Angeles County Museum of Art, *The Vessel as Metaphor: Southern California 1950–1980.*

1986   Exhibition at Fresno, California, Art Center and Museum, *Beatrice Wood—A Legend.*

One-person exhibitions at Garth Clark Gallery, Los Angeles, and Hilberry Gallery, Ann Arbor, Michigan.

1987   "Special People . . . Beatrice Wood," a thirty-minute documentary, wins the gold medal for best biography in the thirtieth annual International Film and TV Festival of New York.

1988   One-person exhibition of drawings at Galleria Civica D'Arte Moderna, Palazzo dei Diamanti, Ferrara, Italy.

INDEX

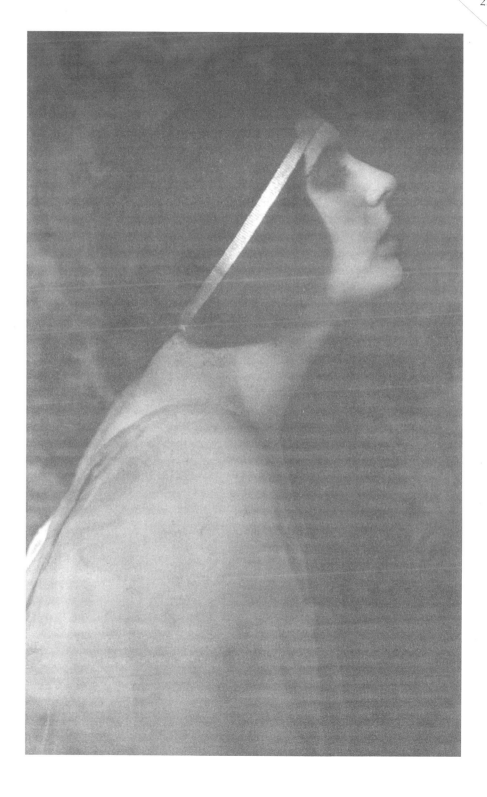

Rebellious, radical, and romantic, Beatrice Wood defied propriety to become a true national treasure. Born in San Francisco in 1893, she studied and acted in Paris during her early twenties. She returned to New York in 1914 where she became romantically involved with the Dadaist Marcel Duchamp. Her friends and acquaintances throughout her lifetime included key cultural figures like Constantin Brancusi, Isadora Duncan, Edna St. Vincent Millay, Anais Nin, Krishnamurti, and many others. After a disastrous marriage, financial woes, and a debilitating physical affliction, at the age of 40 she studied ceramics and went on to become one of the major ceramicists of the 20th century. Her work became increasingly daring and experimental, leading to the creation—in her nineties—of her signature pieces. She continued to work well past age 100.

Photo by Jesse Tarbox Beals